Hiking
the
Escalante

*A wilderness guide
to an exciting land of buttes,
arches, alcoves, amphitheatres
and deep canyons*

To Linda Schnabel
a longtime friend
a great hiking companion
and a fine artist.

Hiking
the
Escalante

by **Rudi Lambrechtse**

Drawings by Linda Schnabel
Maps by Jenny Billideau

Wasatch Publishers, Inc.
Salt Lake City, Utah
1985

Copyright © 1985
Wasatch Publishers, Inc.
4647 Idlewild Road
Salt Lake City, Utah 84124
All rights reserved.
Library of Congress No.: 84-63000
ISBN: 0-915272-27-X

Second Printing 1986

ACKNOWLEDGEMENTS

Many people helped make this project a reality. Special thanks go to Jenny Billideau, who drew the maps, Bonnie Walker, who edited the manuscript, Kathy Graham, who did the typing, and Katie Gooby, who introduced me to the publisher.

Without the willing aid of the people in the Federal agencies who administer the land, this book would not have been completed. For their added help, specific recognition is given to Tom Gillette, Tina Marie Gornick, and Bob McCord. For helping me keep a proper perspective, thanks go to Glenn Sherrill.

It is a happy note that ideas on the direction of this book were a shared experience between the author and the publisher. For his continued support, thanks go to Mel Davis. Besides, he's a fun hiking companion.

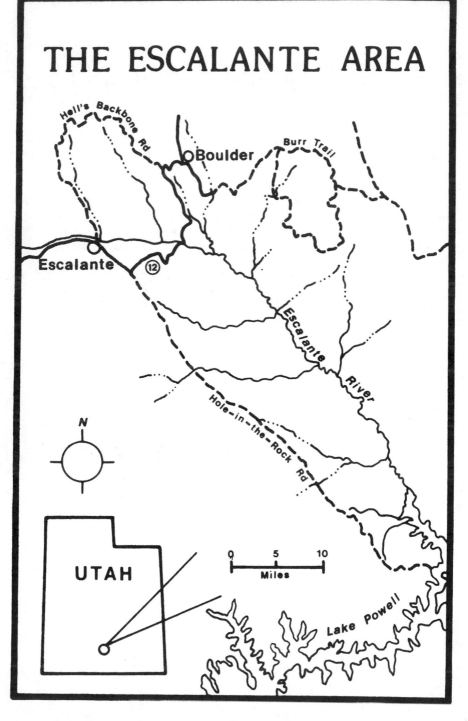

THE ESCALANTE AREA

Hell's Backbone Rd

Boulder

Burr Trail

Escalante

12

Escalante River

Hole-in-the-Rock Rd

N

UTAH

0   5   10
Miles

Lake Powell

CONTENTS

FOREWORD

There is a danger in writing a guidebook that the increased use will destroy those values that attracted one to the area in the first place. There are two reasons for believing that this will not occur here. First is the hope that the comments about minimum impact camping will be taken to heart. As more people use the same area, the greater the need becomes to reduce or eliminate the evidence of your visit. Secondly, having enjoyed the scenic wonders and revelled in the wilderness experience, they will add their voice to those who are working to have this area protected as designated wilderness.

There is a growing realization that we are part of, and not above, the web of interactions that bind this earth. The idea and practice of ecological consciousness is the essence of this book. When this growing awareness is expressed in social and political action, it speaks from a broader perspective than the narrowly perceived user world of the backpacker.

The Escalante canyons remain a vibrant, spacious, and intact ecosystem. Wallace Stegner recognized the unique values of this area when he called it part of "the geography of hope." Come and share it in the same vein.

Publisher's Note:

There are many conflicting opinions on how to write a wilderness guide. Some say there should be no guides nor even maps. "Let the hikers wander and enjoy the adventure of finding their own way and discovering the beauties for themselves." On the other end of the spectrum there are those who would want every step and corner described. We have taken a course somewhere between these two. Realizing that there are virtually no marked trails in this country (mostly only canyons that wander and have many intersections, defying anyone to write explicitly clear directions), we have written clear instructions as to how to get started on the route and then directions helping one to follow along the route, giving choices of side canyons along the way, and sometimes alternate endings. Some of the hikes will be easy for the beginner to follow. Some, only the most experienced should attempt. EVERYONE should realize that this is desert country and can be extremely dangerous for the inexperienced or careless hiker.

The U.S.G.S. maps covering each hike are listed at the beginning of each trail description. These are for sale at the National Park Service office in Escalante. The B.L.M. office next door has an excellent map of the entire area. It is imperative that these maps be used on the more difficult hikes

— Melvin E. Davis

CHAPTER 1

WALKING SOFTLY IN THE WILDERNESS

After two summers as a trail guide, the feeling has been strongly reinforced that the most valuable tool to take into a wilderness setting is the proper attitude. As necessary as skills and good equipment are, that willingness to go into the unknown with an open and receptive outlook will go a long way toward creating a rewarding experience.

Hiking in the Escalante canyons is very different from hiking on a trail. Although there are places where use has created a noticeable way, most hikes involve a certain amount of route selection. In an attempt to minimize your impact, use existing paths wherever possible. In canyons, hike in the bottom near the stream so the next period of high water will erase your footprints. Cutting across benches or terraces can damage fragile desert soils and vegetation and can lead to severe erosion problems. In sandy areas, avoid walking on those black areas of cryptogamic soil. This symbiotic algal and fungal covering, which looks like miniature castles, helps to stabilize the soil. The black ridges take years to form and once this bond with the soil is broken, erosion occurs rapidly.

Appreciation of the wilderness ethic requires the careful disposal of human waste products. There are two requirements in selecting a site. First, you need to be at least 300 feet from a water source and above the high water mark. This is essential for protecting that most valuable of resources. Second, get away from the potential camping spot. Many a trip has been spoiled by the indiscriminate remains of previous hikers. Dig a shallow hole, six to eight inches deep. CAREFULLY burn the toilet paper and then cover the spot. Don't burn the toilet paper if vegetation and wind conditions present any fire hazard.

What is more traditional than a campfire? Yet the arrival at that perfect campsite can be ruined by the numerous fire rings already there. When you hike in the spring and the fall, the need for warmth can easily be provided for by extra clothing and a good supper. The reality that a campfire is not a necessity is a difficult ethic to convey. Hopefully the reason you are here is because this area offers unique wilderness experiences. On a more practical level, evaluate the time spent gathering firewood, digging a pit, burning your dinner, etc., compared to spending that time reading, listening, and observing. Due to the damage associated with campfires, the National Park Service is considering establishment of "stoves only" zones in fragile or heavily used parts of the canyon system. If you are thinking of having a campfire, check with them before entering the area.

If you do build a fire, use an existing firesite and collect only dead and down wood. If camping in an area without any existing fire rings, select a spot below the high water line and do not line your fire with rocks. Let the fire die down to white ash and try to time your camp departure so you can leave a dead fire without having to douse it with water or sand. This will prevent the buildup of charcoal and ash residue which has become such a problem in some parts of the canyon.

Bring a star guide. One of the treats of camping in overhangs is that you can focus on different portions of the sky on successive nights.

A group limit of twelve has been implemented for that portion of the canyons managed by the NPS. Eight seems like a much more reasonable number. With a smaller group it is easier to find a place to camp and deal with all the rest of those interpersonal actions.

Let's not belabor the point: pack it out. Aluminum foil does not burn in a fire. This country looks a lot nicer without leftovers.

Those nighttime noises will be a lot less worrisome if you have secured your food out of the reaches of the night denizens. Most mammals, and especially the rodents, actively forage during the night. By eliminating the possibility of feeding the wild animals, you have food to continue your journey and those wild creatures will remain exactly that. Plan meals so that you do not end up with a lot of leftovers. Food left in camp leads to the proliferation of rodents, ants, flies and other pests.

Water is life. Since you've already paid attention to the proper disposal of your wastes, it is an easy step to not wash your dishes or use soap in the streams. It is advisable to treat all water. This is not the place to get incapacitated. The water temperature must be above 68 °F for chemical

treatment against Giardia to be effective. If it becomes necessary to drink the river water when it is muddy, let the container sit overnight and decant the clear liquid in the morning, then treat with chemicals or by boiling.

Dogs, your friend and mine. Unfortunately they are a disruptive force in the wilderness. They are a threat to wildlife and can be a serious aesthetic intrusion to other hikers. Other pets cause similar problems and all are best left at home.

There are Indian ruins and petroglyphs scattered throughout the canyons. These remains should give you a reason to pause and reflect on the relationships between people and their environment. In order for those that follow to have a similar experience, great care must be exercised in protecting these cultural sites. The Antiquities Act of 1916 and Archeological Resources Protection Act of 1979 make it unlawful to disturb a site or remove any artifacts, but it remains up to the will of the people to safeguard these unique areas. Never walk in, climb on, or camp in any archeological site.

Petrified wood is another of those resources that are best appreciated in situ. The Bureau of Land Management allows a person to collect on Federal land 25 pounds and one piece per day without charge as long as the maximum amount per year does not exceed 250 pounds. This is only if the collecting is for personal use and not bartered or sold to commercial dealers. No collecting is allowed within the Glen Canyon National Recreation Area portion of the Escalante Canyons. To protect the unique visual resource of the Wolverine Natural Area, the area behind the fence has been closed by the BLM.

In order to have a safe and rewarding experience when hiking in this country, a person should carry the ten essentials. (This is not the place to test out new equipment. Be familiar with what you take.) The ten essentials are: a topographic map, a compass, a flashlight with spare parts, extra food and clothing, sun protection, matches, a knife, a signal mirror, a first aid kit, and an emergency shelter. Specific equipment to handle the special requirements of hiking in country with running water is a pair of tennis shoes or good canvas boots.

HIKING SEASON—The best time to hike in the canyons is in the spring or fall. In the summer there is a danger of flash floods, extreme heat, and being eaten alive by deer flies. Although these aggressive insects do not sting, their scissor action to get blood to flow so that they can lap it up will leave a painful wound. The summer is the time to explore the headwaters of some of these drainages and revel in the cool of the Aquarius Plateau. In the winter the river is too cold for wading and walking on ice can be hazardous.

HIKING SAFETY—Conditions can vary radically after a storm, as well as from year to year. It is valuable to first check with the rangers of the proper agency for the area you intend to visit. They can provide updated information about road conditions, give you a free permit, and discuss and compare your hiking ability against your projected route. This also adds to the safety factor since someone will know your itinerary.

HIKING INFORMATION—The BLM and NPS offices are located .8 of a mile west of the center of town on highway 12. Forest Service has an office at 250 W. Main Street. The NPS ranger has topographic maps of the recreation area for sale. Agency addresses are:

Escalante, UT 84726	Telephone - (801)
BLM — P.O. Box 255	826-4291
NPS — P.O. Box 122	826-4315
Forest Service — P.O. Box 246	826-4221

Emergency numbers:

Garfield County Sheriff	676-2678
Glen Canyon Recreation Area	826-4315
Bullfrog District	684-2212

RIVER CONDITIONS—The depth of the river can vary overnight. Spring runoff can occur at any time from March through May. A walking stick can make river crossings safer and easier. Certain side canyons require swimming. The main Escalante River is boulder strewn from Scorpion canyon to just before Stevens. Quicksand is present but does not pose a serious hazard. Usually you won't sink above your knees and extraction is simple. Quicksand poses a greater hazard to cattle. Flashfloods can occur with little warning. Seek high ground and wait for the water to recede.

CATTLE—Most of the area is grazed by cattle. (Cattle grazing has been a long time traditional use of the area.). Antagonizing the cattle and their owners will not foster a favorable local attitude towards backpackers. The rule for cattle gates is to close them after passing through. Be aware of pushing cattle, which is inadvertently driving them ahead of you as you hike. Go slowly around them. There are times when cattle are not found in the canyons. You might want to plan your trip around those brought in the first of November and removed March 31st. Along the river and lower Harris Wash cattle are present from the first of September to June 15. In Scorpion and Coyote Gulches, cattle arrive the first of October and leave June 15. In the summer cattle are grazed on the Aquarius and Kaiparowits Plateaus.

If you discover a dead cow on your hike, get close enough to identify the color of the ear tag and remember the general location. When you give this information to the NPS or BLM, they will know which rancher to contact for the removal of that cow.

FACILITIES—The town of Escalante has two groceries stores, two gas stations, four motels, one restaurant, and a hamburger stand that is open from April through October. You need to bring all of your own basic equipment. There's camping and showers at the Petrified Forest State Park two miles west of town. The BLM has a campground at Calf Creek 15 miles east of town.

The town of Boulder has two gas stations with attached grocery stores. There is one motel and one place to eat. The Anasazi State Park has information and there is a small trailer park next to it.

Waterfall in Deep Creek

Mamie Creek

16

Old brick home in Escalante

CHAPTER 2
HISTORY OF THE AREA

The earliest records were left by the Anasazi Indians. Remains of their brief occupation can be found throughout the area. Their history is dealt with in greater detail in Chapter 5.

The first recorded visit to the area by white people occurred in 1866. An uprising of Paiutes against the Mormon settlements of southern Utah and northern Arizona became known as the Black Hawk War. A group of territorial militia were called into the field and pursued the Indians. Led by Captain James Andrus, the cavalry left Kanab and traveled in a northeasterly direction. They went as far as the summit of Boulder Mountain on the eastern end of the Aquarius Plateau, crossing the upper tributaries of the Escalante River. Convinced that the Indians were safely out of southern Utah, they returned by the same route. Adjutant Franklin B. Woolley sketched a map and wrote the report of the expedition. He named the upper valley of the Escalante River "Potato Valley" because they found wild tubers growing there. His early description accurately defines the country as "cut up in all directions by these narrow deep perpendicular crevices, some of which are hundreds of feet in depth and but a rod or two in width."

John Wesley Powell led expeditions down the Colorado River in 1869 and 1871, but they did not see the mouth of the Escalante River. Members of the second expedition, led by Powell's brother-in-law Almon H. Thompson, traversed the upper tributaries of the Escalante River in 1872 in route to retrieving a boat cached at the mouth of the Dirty Devil River. The deep gorges of the Escalante canyons also forced these explorers to detour to the north and climb the Aquarius Plateau before continuing east. Thompson realized that the drainage they were skirting was not the Dirty Devil and they had discovered a totally new river.

The name Escalante was recommended by Thompson to a group of Mormons he met at Pine Creek in 1875. Escalante was the name of one of the Franciscan friars who searched for a new route from Sante Fe to Monterey. In that epic journey of 1776, they explored a great deal of Utah. They passed far south of the country named after him, crossing the Colorado River in lower Glen Canyon.

For the rest of 1875, those early settlers worked on a road over Table Cliff Mountain into the upper Escalante basin. The following year work was begun on irrigation canals and a townsite was laid out. Escalante's settlement differed from the pattern of other southern Utah communities where the instigating factor was a call from the church authorities. The Mormon pioneers who settle Escalante were searching for a place to settle that had less severe weather than Panguitch. The orderly organization of the townsite and the placement of the settlement near the headwaters of a river was the Mormon tradition. Lumber and dairy cattle were two early industries. At the turn of the century many fine brick homes were built, giving the town a distinctive look.

In the fall of 1879 the Hole-in-the-Rock expedition passed through the small community on its way to settle on the San Juan River in southeastern Utah. Scouts had explored longer routes through Green River or Flagstaff, but the most direct and unexplored way was chosen. Staying west of the Escalante canyons, these pioneers blasted and constructed a precarious route for their 80 wagons and livestock through a narrow defile looking down into the Colorado River. Dance Hall Rock became the focal point for dancing and socializing while the road was being constructed. After safely getting the wagons down and across the river, the expedition struggled on through even more difficult country. They arrived exhausted at the site of Bluff, six months after they started.

In November of 1934, a young artist came to the Escalante canyons with a different vision. Everett Ruess had wandered extensively in the canyons of the southwest since 1930. With a pair of burros to carry his food and art supplies, Everett went into the slick rock maze of the lower canyons. He was never seen again. A search party the next year located his burros in Davis Gulch. Several NEMO inscriptions were found on the canyon walls. Everett had a history of using pseudonyms. NEMO is the latin word for "nobody" used by the Greek Odysseus to trick a man-eating giant. It could also refer to Captain Nemo in Jules Verne's *Twenty Thousand Leagues*

Under the Sea, another person who was trying to escape from civilization.

While speculation on Ruess' disappearance continues, especially since none of his outfit was ever found, his legacy of wilderness exploration and appreciation lives on. As part of a letter written shortly before he vanished, Everett reiterates his reason for being there: "As to when I shall visit civilization, it will not be soon, I think. I have not tired of the wilderness; rather I enjoy its beauty and the vagrant life I lead, more keenly all the time. I prefer the saddle to the streetcar and the star-sprinkled sky to a roof, the obscure and difficult trail, heading into the unknown, to any paved highway, and the deep peace of the wild to the discontent bred by cities. Do you blame me then for staying here, where I feel that I belong and am one with the world around me?"

The 1930s were also a period of construction by the Civilian Conservation Corps. If the town of Escalante was difficult to get to due to the broken terrain, Boulder was at the edge of the world. The men of the CCC, based at Hungry Creek 15 miles north of Escalante, built a road across Hell's Backbone to Boulder. The strip of road that wound precariously around the head of Death Hollow was coined "the poison road, one drop sure death." The CCC also built a recreation camp at Posy Lake and the dugway that climbs up the canyon wall by Calf Creek. This became part of the new highway to Boulder in 1940. Boulder thus ceased to be the last packhorse town.

In the 1950s, uranium exploration pushed roads into many areas. The Bureau of Land Management and Boulder stockmen worked together to construct a road from Boulder through Long Canyon into the rangeland of the Flats. This road is now part of the Burr Trail. It also provided access to the uranium mines in the Circle Cliffs.

The scenic marvels of the canyons, especially the many arches and natural bridges, slowly became known to the outside world through articles written in the National Geographic. Most of these lower canyons were inundated when Glen Canyon Dam was completed in 1964.

In recent years, the diversity of hiking challenges has drawn greater numbers of backpackers into this area. It is still very similar to the description given by Clarence Dutton in 1880: "Maze of cliffs and terraces lined with stratification, of crumbling buttes, red and white domes, rock platforms gashed with profound canyons, burning plains barren even of sage — all glowing with bright color and flooded with blazing sunlight."

Era	Period	Group	Formation	Thickness (feet)
MESOZOIC	CRETACEOUS		Kaiparowits Fm	2700 feet
			Wahweap Ss	1250
			Straight Cliffs Fm	1100
			Tropic Shale	600
			Dakota Ss	40-100
	JURASSIC		Morrison Fm	0-365
		San Rafael Group	Summerville Fm	0-145
			Entrada Ss	600-750
			Carmel Fm	200-400
	TRIASSIC	Glen Canyon Group	Navajo Ss	600-1500
			Kayenta Fm	50-300
			Wingate Ss	300
			Chinle Fm	400
			Shinarump Mbr	0-200

Geologic History of Utah, L. F. Hintze

Formations around Coyote Gulch

CHAPTER 3

GEOLOGY

The Escalante Canyons are part of a large basin bounded by the Circle Cliffs and the Waterpocket fold to the East, the Straight Cliffs to the West, and the Aquarius Plateau to the North. The Circle Cliffs and Waterpocket Fold were uplifted during the Laramide Orogeny, a period of violent geological activity that occurred 50-80 million years before the present. The Waterpocket Fold is an extensive monocline, or buckling of the earth, that extends 80 miles from the Fremont River to Lake Powell. The Circle Cliffs are found at the western edge of the Waterpocket Fold. They have eroded into massive cliffs. The Straight Cliffs are the eastern escarpment of the Kaiparowits Plateau that extend for 50 miles from the town of Escalante to Lake Powell. The Kaiparowits and Aquarius Plateaus were also uplifted during the Laramide Orogeny. The Aquarius Plateau is a vast tableland capped by recent volcanic and glacial deposits of Cenozoic age. This plateau rises over 10,000 feet above sea level. With the uplift of the Circle Cliffs, Waterpocket Fold, Kaiparowits and Aquarius Plateaus, the increased erosional forces cut the modern drainage pattern of the Escalante Canyons.

21

The rocks exposed in the Escalante area were deposited during the last two eras of geological time, the Cenozoic (0-65 m.y.b.p.) and the Mesozoic (65-230 m.y.b.p.). The Mesozoic Era has been divided into three periods: the Cretaceous (65-135 m.y.b.p.), the Jurassic (135-180 m.y.b.p.), and the Triassic (180-230 m.y.b.p.).

The rock layers exposed in the Escalante Canyons were deposited during the Jurassic and Triassic Periods. The Morrison Formation, of upper Jurassic age, was deposited by streams wandering through lowlands. The sandstone and siltstone colors vary from tan to gray, purple, green, or maroon. Dinosaur fossils are frequently found in this formation. This colorful cliff former is found west of the town of Escalante and near the base of the Straight Cliffs.

Sedimentary rocks of the San Rafael Group, or middle to late Jurassic age, consist of the Summerville Formation, Entrada Sandstone, and the Carmel Formation. The Summerville Formation varies from brown siltstones and mudstones left by the retreating Curtis Sea to yellow sandstones formed from dunes next to the tidal flats. It forms ledgy slopes to cliffs found near the base of the Straight Cliffs. The Entrada Sandstone is a reddish-tan, crossbedded, cliff-forming sandstone. Dance Hall Rock and Chimney Rock are composed of Entrada Sandstone. The Carmel Formation consists of reddish shales, mudstones, siltstones, and gypsum. The Carmel forms a series of ledges and slopes. It is found along the Hole-in-the-Rock road at Red Breaks and the head of Twentyfive Mile Wash.

The majority of the Escalante Canyons are carved into rocks of the Glen Canyon Group, of Triassic-Jurassic age. This group consists of the Navajo Sandstone, the Kayenta Formation, and the Wingate Sandstone. The Navajo Sandstone, youngest of the Glen Canyon Group, is a white to brown, crossbedded, sandstone cliff former, that was accumulated by an eolian (windblown) environment near a marine environment. This rock erodes into fins, domes, buttes, and imposing cliffs. Arches are usually found near the base of the Navajo where it is in contact with the underlying Kayenta. The Navajo Sandstone is exposed in the Escalante Canyon walls from the town of Escalante to Horse Canyon. The Kayenta Formation forms a series of tan to maroon ledges and slopes of sandstones and siltstones. The Kayenta represents a return to fluvial or stream environments. It is found in the canyon walls of the Escalante River from Horse Canyon to Coyote Gulch. The Wingate Sandstone, oldest of the Glen Canyon Series, forms reddish-brown, cross-stratified, sandstone cliffs of eolian origin. This sandstone is subject to conchoidal fracturing such as those seen in East Moody Canyon. The Wingate is found from Choprock Bench to Coyote Gulch.

The most colorful rock formation in the area is the Triassic Chinle Formation, composed of red, brown, purple, gray, and occasionally pale green shales. This highly erodable formation contains petrified wood that was deposited along the floodplains of streams. The colors are derived from the oxides of the iron-bearing minerals. This slope former is exposed along the base of the Circle Cliffs and at the base of the Escalante Canyon walls from Moody to Stevens Canyon.

The Shinarump Conglomerate is the basal member of the Chinle Formation and is exposed as a ledge of gray, resistant, coarse sandstone and conglomerate. A fluvial deposit, the sediment was formed by the erosion of the ancestoral Rockies to the east and south. The name Shinar means wolf in Paiute and rump means posterior in English. The concentration of organic debris occurred in point-bar deposits (the inner bends of meandering streams). This debris induced uranium mineralization, adding special interest to where this layer is exposed.

Death Hollow

23

Cryptogamic soil

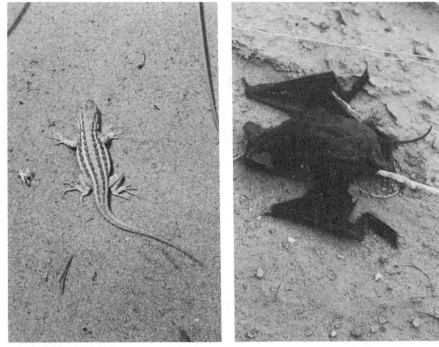

Eastern fence lizard

Mexican free-tailed bat

CHAPTER 4
NATURAL HISTORY

The Escalante canyons are part of the Colorado plateau province. While the canyons themselves are in a basin, higher land bounds the area on three sides. This broken topography creates a high degree of diversity in both the plant communities and the animal life. The top of the Aquarius Plateau, which forms the northern boundary of the Escalante basin, is over 11,000 feet. Where Lake Powell backs up into the lower canyons, the elevation is around 3,700 feet above sea level.

Besides elevation, other factors such as temperature, available moisture, soil makeup, and slope direction affect plant distribution. Mammals are not as strongly affected by such variables, but they too have adapted to the wide range of conditions found here. While those animals found at the higher elevations have to deal with snow and cold, those living in the lower desert have to contend with extreme summer heat.

The area contains approximately 66 species of mammals, 150 + bird species, five types of toads and frogs, nine lizards, and eleven snake species. Three of these snake species are poisonous. The National Park Service has checklists for the birds and mammals of Glen Canyon National Recreation Area. While not all of the species listed are found around Escalante, they are a valuable reference.

In an attempt to place the plants in an ecological setting, a community or association will be described. For orientation, this community description will be tied to a distinct topographic feature or a specific geographical area.   This will hopefully make it easier to understand   your surroundings.

The northern edge of the Escalante Canyons is the Aquarius Plateau. This relatively level area of lakes, meadows and trees rises to over 11,000 feet. The southern escarpment is cut by streams which provide a continuous source of water for the Escalante River. The lakes are stocked with cutthroat, brook, and rainbow trout. The upper part of the plateau falls in the Subalpine or Hudsonian Zone (approximately 9,500'-11,500' elevation). Also known as the spruce-fir association, Englemann spruce and subalpine fir are the key species. Myrtle blueberry, wolf currant, and wax flower are common shrubs. Fireweed, silvery lupine, fleabane, and harebell are common meadow flowers. Mule deer, northern pocket gophers, and yellow bellied marmots are some of the mammals. Hawks and golden eagles fly overhead, while mountain bluebirds and Cassin's finches are seen at the edge of the meadows.

Below the volcanic rim of the Plateau is the fir-aspen or Canadian Zone, which covers from 8,000' to 9,500' in elevation. Blue spruce, quaking aspen, and Douglas fir are the dominant tree species. Common shrubs include Utah honeysuckle, elderberry, common juniper, wild raspberry, and gooseberry. Bebb and Scouler willow thickets crowd the streambanks. Beaver dams abound. Summer flowers are cranesbill, western yarrow, Columbia monkshood, sego lily, mountain gentian, and Indian paintbrush.

Coyote tracks

Velvetgrass, downy brome, and the introduced wheatgrass also provide ground cover.

A variety of butterflies can be seen in the late summer. Aquatic birds such as teals, mallards, pintails, and coots utilize the marshy lakes. Broad-tailed hummingbirds, tree swallows, house wrens, yellow-bellied sapsuckers, flickers, and red-tailed hawks adorn the sky. The noisy spruce squirrel, Colorado and least chipmunks, and the golden-mantled ground squirrel are common rodents. Elk, mule-deer, coyote, and beaver are among the other more visible mammals.

The next distinct topographic feature is the steep-walled canyons that drain this plateau. These include Pine Creek, Death Hollow, and Sand Creek. Portions of the Hell's Backbone road also traverse this vegetation grouping, known as the Transition Zone. The key species is the ponderosa pine tree, found roughly in the elevation range from 6,500' to 8,000'.

Douglas fir, Gamble oak, rocky mountain juniper, thin leaf alder, and red-osier dogwood are also found here. Shrub species are pointleaf manzanita and Utah serviceberry. Shrubby cinquefoil, Fendler rose, common aster, and wheeler thistle are common understory perennials. Grasses include redtop, wildoat, and bluegrass.

Mountain lion, mule deer, porcupines, chipmunks, and the golden-mantled ground squirrel are important mammals. Many birds are found in this forest, including the noisy crested Stellar's jay. Mountain and western bluebirds, mountain and black-capped chickadees, Grace's warblers, western tanagers, pygmy nuthatches, broad-tailed hummingbirds, blue grouse, and a variety of owls utilize this habitat. Belted kingfishers and water ouzels are found next to the streams.

The western edge of the Escalante basin is framed by the Straight Cliffs, the eastern edge of the Kaiparowits Plateau. With the exception of Harris Wash and Collet Wash, which originate on the plateau, the rest of the streams running eastward to the Escalante River are basin borne. The pinyon-juniper woodland type is found at the base of the Straight Cliffs. These trees are also found at the start of the Hole-in-the-Rock road and along the drainages.

The geographical feature below the Straight Cliffs is known as desert flats, and is part of the Northern Desert Shrub Association. Most of the Hole-in-the-Rock road traverses an area of shallow rocky soil, covered by extensive stands of blackbrush. Mormon tea, shadscale, and broom snakeweed are other common shrubs. Around Fortymile ridge, purple or desert sage, which is really a mint, can put on a bright blue and purple display in the spring. Where the soils are deeper and sandier, there is an increase in Indian ricegrass, dropseed, three-awn, galleta, and needle and thread grass. Narrowleaf yucca, opuntia or prickly pear, and evening primrose also dot the landscape.

Characteristic mammals of these desert flats are the coyote, blacktailed jackrabbits, Audubon cottontails, deer mice, northern grasshopper mice, little pocket mice, and Ord's kangaroo rats. In this warm climate are found such lizards as the western whiptail, the side-blotched, and leopard. Loggerheaded shrikes, horned larks, and common nighthawks frequent this

Ord's kangaroo rat

area. The black-throated sparrow resides in the blackbrush flats.

The Circle Cliffs are an imposing geological feature of striking colors and sharp relief on the east side of the Escalante basin. At the base of the Circle Cliffs and on the mesas and benchlands the ground is covered with pinyon and juniper trees. Local patches of Gamble oak and rabbitbrush are interspersed. Big sage occupies the floor of the Circle Cliffs basin. The canyons that drain the Circle Cliffs contain Mormon tea, yucca, serviceberry, oak, silver buffaloberry, and Palmer's penstemon.

Bighorn sheep have been reintroduced into the area, while the most common large mammal is the mule deer. Desert cottontails, black-tailed jackrabbits, Colorado chipmunks, rock squirrels, desert woodrats, white-tailed antelope squirrels, deer mice, and Ord's kangaroo rats are common. Coyotes are ubiquitous.

Typical birds are the mourning dove, scrub jay, raven, Say's phoebe, vesper sparrow, blue-gray gnatcatcher, ash-throated fly-catcher, rock wren, house finch, green-tailed towhee, pinyon jay, black-throated gray warbler, plain titmouse, and common bush tit.

The area around the town of Escalante is also part of the pinyon-juniper woodland. It is known as the pygmy forest because the trees seldom grow over thirty feet. This Upper Sonoron Zone ranges from 4,500 to 6,000 feet above sea level. In the meadows around town are western meadowlarks, magpies, Bullock's orioles, Brewer's blackbirds, and redwinged blackbirds.

The Escalante River drops 2,000 feet between town and Lake Powell. A general ecological division can be made between the habitat of the canyon shelves and benches and the riparian habitat. This distinction also applies to the side canyons with flowing water.

Starting by the town, the pinyon pine and Utah junipers of the pygmy forest dominate the canyon slopes. Where the benches have accumulated sandy soil, old man sage and joint fir are found. If these areas of soil are

28

somewhat sheltered, single leaf ash, cliff-rose, roundleaf buffaloberry, Gamble oak, box elder, serviceberry, squawbush, fremont barberry, desert ceanothus, and Apache-plume appear. Blackbrush and big sage also intrude into this zone and can constitute important localized areas of shrub cover. The creeping vine that has distinctive white furry balls in the fall is western virgin's bower. The hedgehog cactus has a strikingly attractive red flower. Other colorful perennials are sacred datura, paintbrush, skyrocket gilia, and scarlet bugler.

Mammals frequently found but not necessarily seen include mountain lions, mule deer, gray foxes, coyotes, pinyon mice, deer mice, desert woodrats, and Ord's kangaroo rats. A variety of bat species range over the area.

When the benches become a dominant part of the canyon topography below The Gulch, big sage becomes the dominant plant. Rabbitbrush and greasewood are also found. Globe mallow adds its orange hue in the summer. Galleta, grama, and squirreltail are common perennial grasses. These plants are one grouping of the Northern Desert Shrub Association.

Frequently seen birds include the scrub jay, ash-throated flycatcher, common bush tit, white-throated swift, canyon wren, and rock wren.

In the sand dunes around the Moody Canyons, Indian rice grass and narrow leaf yuccas are common. The colorful shales that appear further down canyon support very few plants, but one of the most conspicious is the desert trumpet, with its inflated stems.

The other major habitat in the canyons is the flowing waterway, or the riparian zone.

Along the stream the Fremont cottonwood is the most frequently seen tree. Willows and salt cedar or tamarisk crowd the streambanks and the alluvial plains. Right at the stream edge, sedges, scouring rushes, saltgrass, and common horsetails abound.

Common mammals along the waterway are beaver and muskrat. Also found in the canyon are the Colorado chipmunk, cliff chipmunk, rock squirrel, brush mouse, pinyon mouse, deer mouse, and desert wood rat.

The great blue heron, snowy egret, and a variety of ducks can be found along the river. Along the canyon bottom may be seen Bullock's oriole, house finch, yellow warbler, ash-throated flycatcher, black-headed grosbeak, broad tailed hummingbirds, and western wood pewee.

The Rocky Mountain toad, red spotted toad, Great Basin spade-foot, wandering garter snake, striped whipsnake and gopher snake are common. Western leopard frogs are common along the lower Escalante River. The canyon tree frog is common in potholes of the lower side canyons.

A special habitat found in the side canyons occurs where there is water seepage on the cliff. These can occur at any place on the cliff but usually are found near the base. They add a spectacular contrast, especially when they are found in the over-arching amphitheaters carved out of the cliff faces. This specialized community is known as the hanging garden community, and is only found in this mezic environment. The most common plant found there is maidenhair fern. Mosses and common liverworts also grow into luxuriant mats on these walls. The giant helleborine orchid, red monkey flower, cliff columbine, cardinal flower, elegant death camas, and Rydberg thistle all add color to the display.

Petroglyphs

CHAPTER 5
PREHISTORY

By Larry Davis
Park Manager
Anasazi State Park

The earliest dates for man in Utah have been obtained from excavations of cave sites in the northwestern part of the State as well as two sites in southern Utah, and place man in Utah before 8,000 years ago.

The culture most evident in southern Utah is known as the Anasazi culture and existed from about the time of Christ until A.D. 1300. During this time, the Anasazi culture became widespread throughout the four corners area of the Southwest. The culture has been divided into successive time periods, the earliest of which is called Basketmaker and the later, Pueblo.

The Escalante Canyons and much of the surrounding area was settled by a group or groups of Anasazi who moved to this previously unoccupied area from the San Juan River country to the southeast. Probable factors for the settlement of the area were an abundance of arable land, permanent supply of water, presence of materials for buildings, pottery, clothing, and tools, supply of firewood, and an abundance of game animals in the vicinity.

The Kayenta branch of Anasazi culture, which centered in northeastern Arizona, was the basic ingredient of this culture. Minor influences are also noted from the Mesa Verde and Chaco branches of the Anasazi culture as well as the Fremont culture to the north and east.

The archaeological evidence indicates that the area was occupied for a relatively short period of time, between A.D. 1050-1200.

These people were farmers, raising corn, beans, and squash. They supplemented these foodstuffs by gathering seeds, berries, and nuts. They also utilized small and large game animals for food.

The canyons were probably a year-round home for some of the Anasazi inhabitants and a seasonal home for others.

Many of the modern Pueblo Indians living in New Mexico and Arizona are the probable descendants of the Anasazi. The Escalante River area, like much of the entire Anasazi area, was never again occupied by farming Indians after it was abandoned by the Anasazi.

As you hike the many canyons of the Escalante River you will see the remnants of the Anasazi culture. These take the form of rock art (pictographs and petroglyphs), ruins of habitation and storage structures, and simple camp sites and use areas.

Both State and Federal law prohibit the appropriation, excavation, injury, or destruction of any prehistoric or historic ruin or monument, or any object of antiquity. Violation and conviction under either law is subject to a fine or imprisonment, or both.

Moqui house

Petroglyphs

Unfortunately, a great many people are ignoring the antiquity laws and are destroying many of the archaeological sites in the area through unauthorized and unscientific excavations. The "pothunting" activities are conducted by people in order to obtain artifacts to sell to collectors and dealers. In doing so, these people vandalize and forever destroy archaeological sites, making it extremely difficult to obtain scientific information from them. This makes it difficult to add to the already fascinating story of the Anasazi.

When hiking these canyons, we ask that when you find archaeological sites or objects of antiquity, you observe them and take a while to reflect back on these people and their ability to survive and adapt to this area. We would then invite you to leave these sites or objects as you found them so that others may enjoy.

A collection of Kayenta Anasazi artifacts as well as an Anasazi village may be seen at the museum and archaeological site at Anasazi State Park in Boulder, Utah. The museum is open seven days a week.

HELL'S BACKBONE
ROAD

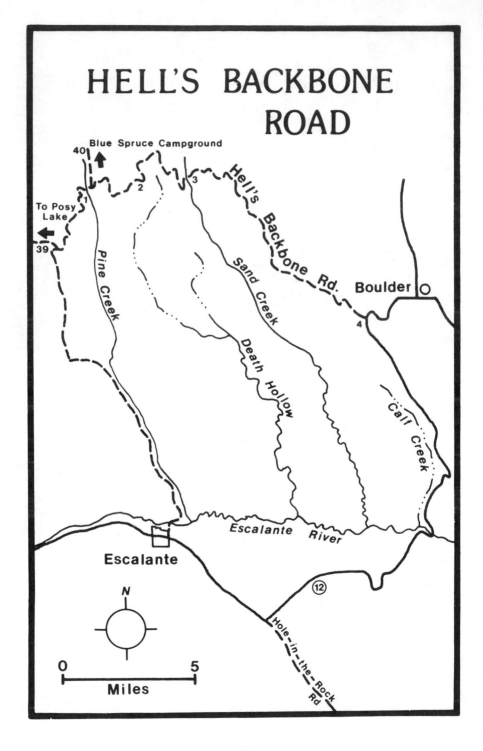

Blue Spruce Campground

40

Hell's Backbone Rd.

To Posy Lake

39

Pine Creek

Sand Creek

Death Hollow

Boulder

Calf Creek

Escalante River

Escalante

N

12

Hole-in-the-Rock Rd

0   5
Miles

CHAPTER 6
ROAD LOGS AND TRAIL DESCRIPTIONS

I. HELL'S BACKBONE

This highly scenic road, built by the CCC in the 1930s, connected Escalante and Boulder. Winding through the forest, there are excellent views of the slickrock country. The Hell's Backbone bridge crosses a small saddle between two canyons of colorful sandstone. The aspen add additional color in the fall. For the hiker, this road provides access to some of the most challenging hiking found in the area.

Directions (L) and (R) are given from Escalante. They would be opposite coming from Boulder.

MILES		DESCRIPTION
From Boulder	From Escalante	
40.1	0.0	Middle of town
39.7	0.4	Turn left for Hell's Backbone road
39.2	0.9	Escalante River crossing
32.1	8.0	Turnoff (R) to the Box. This is the exit for TRAIL 1 where Pine Creek cuts through the Escalante Monocline.
25.8	14.3	Turnoff (L) to Posy Lake and Loa 1.3 — Hog Spring Ranch Road (L) 2.1 — Posy Lake Campground (L) **TRAIL 39 — Posy Lake Lookout**
21.3	18.8	**TRAIL 1 — Pine Creek**
21.1	19.0	Turnoff (L) to Blue Spruce Campground 0.5 — Blue Spruce Campground 0.8 — Cowpuncher Guard Station 1.6 — Road (L) 1.8 — **TRAIL 40 — Jacob's Reservoir**
17.8	22.3	Road (L) Go straight on the smaller road. The road is graveled to this point.
16.0	24.1	**TRAIL 2 — Death Hollow**

14.7	25.4	Hell's Backbone bridge. When the CCC built this road in the 1930s, the crew working from the east had premade the bridge so it would be ready when the two crews met. The views below are spectacular. The road is narrow as you head down. Rocky mountain juniper with its droopy branches and manzanita line the road.
11.8	28.3	**TRAIL 3 — Sand Creek.** The road is graveled again from here to Highway 12.
9.5	30.6	Lake Creek
7.3	32.8	Mount Ogden appears straight ahead.
6.5	33.6	Navajo Mountain and the Straight Cliffs are visible in the distance.
1.3	38.8	Big Hollow
0.2	39.9	**TRAIL 4 — Boulder Mail Trail** takes off on this dirt road.
0.0	40.1	Highway 12. Turn left to go to Boulder and right to Escalante.

II. HIGHWAY 12

This is the main road into Escalante from Bryce. Extended to Boulder in 1940, it is now paved almost all the way to Torrey. There is thus easier access into the canyon country from the north. Earlier wagon roads connecting Boulder and Escalante provide points of interest for the hiker and historian. The self-sufficiency of these two communities has been part of the proud pioneer tradition that helped settle this area.

Directions (L) and (R) are given from Escalante. They would be opposite coming from Torrey.

MILES		**D E S C R I P T I O N**
From Torrey	From Escalante	
66.9	0.0	Road log heading east. Center of town, located at the corner of Main Street and Griffin's Grocery Store.
66.5	0.4	Hell's Backbone road (L)
65.8	1.1	Road (L) It curves past the cemetery and goes to the dump. This road is the exit route for TRAIL 4. There are places to park just past the cattleguard and at the end of the road when it goes past the western edge of the dump.
		TRAIL 5 — Escalante River to Calf Creek

HIGHWAY 12

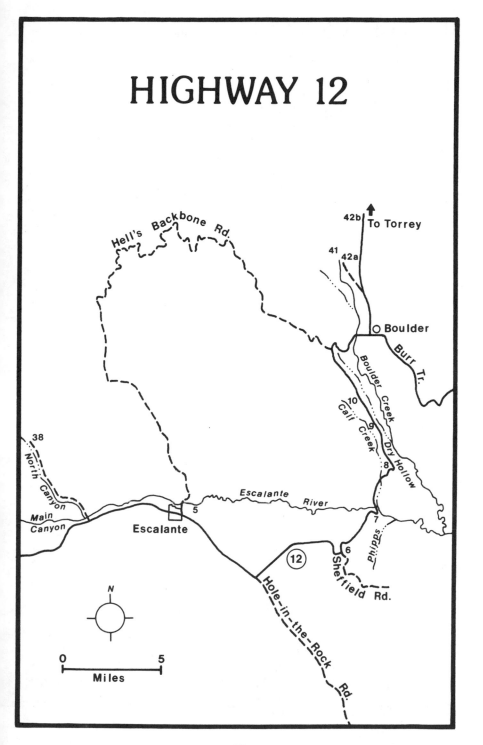

II. HIGHWAY 12 (Continued)

MILES		DESCRIPTION
From Torrey	From Escalante	
64.2	2.7	Airport road (R)
61.8	5.1	Hole-in-the-Rock road (R)
61.4	5.5	Hole-in-the-Rock road (R) accessed from Boulder.
57.5	9.4	Good view (L) of slickrock
56.7	10.2	Overlook (L) with views of the Henry Mountains to the east. The white domeland immediately below you is known locally as Head of the Rocks. A portion of the old Boulder road, known as the "Cream Cellar Route," was constructed to avoid the deep sands of Phipp's Pasture. It was used from 1928-1940 until the present highway was completed.
56.0	10.9	Sheffield road (R). Sam Sheffield was an early settler in the area and constructed this road to get to his homestead on the Escalante River. The main road drops down steeply. **0.3 – TRAIL 6 – Phipps Wash**
55.2	11.7	Look to the right down the narrow slot.
54.9	12.0	Pullout (R) see description with TRAIL 6.
52.7	14.2	Boyton Overlook (L). Good view of the Escalante River.
52.0	14.9	**TRAIL 7 – Escalante River from Calf Creek to Harris Wash.** Road crosses low concrete bridge over the Escalante River.
51.2	15.7	Road crosses Calf Creek.
51.1	15.8	Road (L) with access to Calf Creek and alcove to the west.
50.6	16.3	Calf Creek Campground (L) is maintained by the BLM. **0.4 – TRAIL 8 – Lower Calf Creek Falls**
50.0	16.9	The road climbs sharply through the red Kayenta layer up the side of Haymaker Bench.
48.5	18.4	There is a small arch just left of the road.
47.3	19.6	**TRAIL 9 – Dry Hollow-Boulder Creek**
47.0	19.9	Great views on either side of the road as it crosses the Hogback.
44.6	22.3	**TRAIL 10 – Upper Calf Creek Falls**
42.1	24.8	Hell's Backbone road (L)
41.5	25.4	Excellent view to the right of the head of Dry Hollow.
39.5	27.4	Boulder Creek
38.9	28.0	Boulder. Burr Trail (R). The town of Boulder has two stores that sell gasoline, one motel, and a cafe on the corner of the Burr Trail turnoff and Highway 12.
38.2	28.7	Anasazi State Park (R)

| 33.0 | 33.9 | Garkane Power Plant (L) |

                  1.9 — Haw's pasture road (L). Go right up the King's Pasture road. The gravel ends directly and the road is rocky in places so a slow passage is in order.

                  2.4 — Stay on the main road that goes right.

                  3.2 — Cattleguard

                  5.9 — Road (R). Straight ahead the road deadends. This is a good place to park.

                      0.2 — TRAIL 42a — Deer Creek Lake

                      0.8 — TRAIL 41 — East Boulder Creek

30.6	36.3	Nice stand of aspen
28.1	38.8	**TRAIL 42b — Deer Creek Lake (L).**
26.8	40.1	Point Lookout view point (R). Views of the Circle Cliffs, the Upper Gulch and Steep Creek drainages, and the Henry Mountains.
0.0	66.9	Road continues on to Torrey.

III. BURR TRAIL

This road, not recommended for trailers due to the tight switchbacks through the Waterpocket Fold, provides access to the highly colorful country of the Circle Cliffs. Not passable after a recent storm due to the clay substrate in places, travel to trailheads off this road puts you a long way from civilization. Most of this country was made accessible by the uranium boom of the 1950s.

MILES	DESCRIPTION
0.0	Road going east off of Highway 12 at Boulder is the Burr Trail. This road goes through the Waterpocket Fold, a hundred mile long monocline that is part of Capital Reef National Park.
2.8	End of the pavement. The mesa that was off to the right is an excellent example of the striated crossbedding that occurs in the Navajo sandstone.
6.5	**TRAIL 11 — Deer Creek.** The Bureau of Land Management has a primitive campground on the north side of the road.
10.7	**TRAIL 12 — Upper Gulch**
	TRAIL 13 — The Gulch
12.1	Narrow slot canyon to the north. The road follows Long Canyon. The scenery changes from red to white as the Wingate cliffs dominate.
17.6	Pullout (R). Views of the Circle Cliffs and the Henry Mountains in the distance. The road drops sharply and becomes impassable when wet.

THE BURR TRAIL

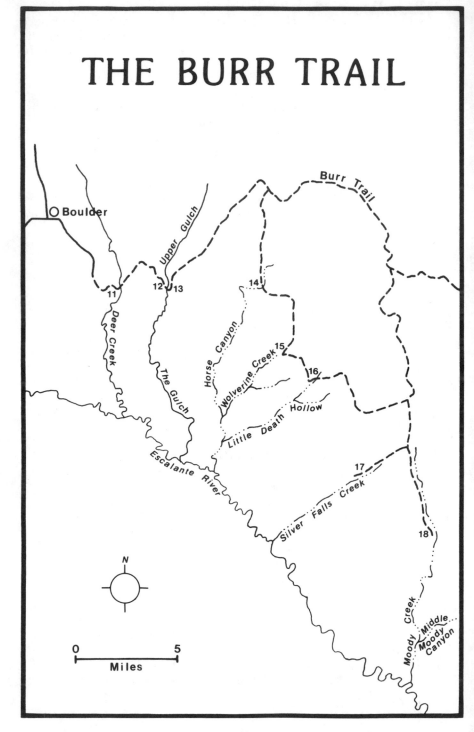

Boulder

Burr Trail

Upper Gulch

11   12 13   14

Deer Creek

The Gulch

Horse Canyon

Wolverine Creek 15

16

Little Death Hollow

Escalante River

Silver Falls Creek   17

18

Moody Creek   Middle Moody Canyon

N

0   5
Miles

III.   BURR TRAIL (Continued)

19.3   Turnoff (R) to Horse Canyon, Wolverine Canyon, Little Death Hollow, Silver Falls Creek, and Moody Canyon.

    5.7 — **TRAIL 14 — Horse Canyon.** The road goes through the bed of the drainage and may be impassable after a heavy rain.

    10.4 — **TRAIL 15 — Wolverine Creek.** The area beyond the fence is part of the Wolverine Natural Area and is closed to petrified wood collection. Massive black petrified logs lie exposed on the pink and purple ground.

    13.2 — **TRAIL 16 — Little Death Hollow.** The topographic map calls this Death Hollow but I have added the "little" to differentiate it from TRAIL 2 coming off the Aquarius Plateau.

    20.3 — The road (L) goes north to the Burr Trail. Road to the right continues on to Moody Canyon.

    23.0 — Turnoff (R) to Silver Falls Creek.

        0.7 — Road (R) goes to a uranium mine.

        1.1 — Road follows the creekbed.

        2.4 — **TRAIL 17 — Silver Falls Creek.** Corral on the right.

    24.0 — Fence

    24.2 — Corral and house

    26.3 — Stock tank (R)

    29.3 — Road goes into the creekbed. Four-wheel drive recommended if you continue further down the wash.

    32.3 — **TRAIL 18 — Moody Canyon.** Corral and line camp (R).

30.2   Turnoff (R) to Silver Falls Creek and Moody Canyon. Road goes 8.4 miles to junction with road coming past Horse Canyon, Wolverine Canyon, and Little Death Hollow.

35.2   Burr Trail cuts through the Waterpocket Fold. Serious switchbacks require slow driving along this stretch.

HOLE-IN-THE-ROCK
ROAD

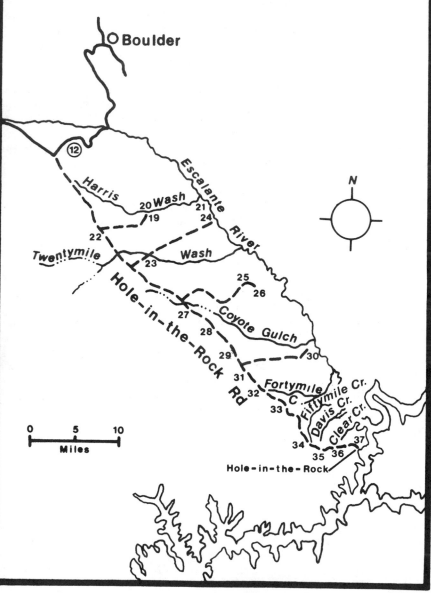

IV. HOLE-IN-THE-ROCK ROAD

This road provides access to the drainages on the west side of the Escalante River and terminates at the historic site of Hole-in-the-Rock. The road follows the general path taken by the San Juan Mission. This group of 250 people, answering the call of the Mormon Church to settle along the San Juan River, passed this way in 1879 and 1880. Overcoming tremendous physical barriers, they blasted a wagon route through a narrow slot at the rim of Glen Canyon. Without the loss of a single wagon they ferried the Colorado River and reached their destination after six months on the road. This is the most popular access to the Escalante Canyons.

MILES	DESCRIPTION
0.0	Turnoff from Highway 12
0.3	Road (R)
0.4	Other road from Highway 12 comes in from left.
0.5	BLM sign
2.5	Go slow because the road curves.
4.4	Alvey Wash crossing
8.2	Cattleguard
8.4	Road (R)
10.8	Turnoff left to Harris Trailhead.

    2.8 — Cattleguard. Take the road to the left. The road winds down the Carmel Formation. It is curvy and is slick when wet.

    4.9 — Road crosses wash

    5.1 — Another wash crossing

    5.3 — Harris Wash and willows visible to the left.

    5.6 — Corral on right — go through the gate.

    6.3 — **TRAIL 19 — Harris Wash**
           TRAIL 20 — Red Breaks

| 12.7 | Road (R) to Devil's Garden at .3 of a mile. |

TRAIL 22 — Devil's Garden

| 17.2 | Egypt Turnoff (L) |

    3.7 — **TRAIL 23 — Twentyfive mile Wash.** Road crosses the drainage.

    4.0 — Juniper drift fence on right.

    6.8 — Sharp turn to the right and the road descends.

    7.0 — Slot side canyon to the right, great for a day hike. Road climbs up the hill.

    8.5 — Egypt sign, stay right.

    9.1 — **TRAIL 24 — Fence Canyon**

18.4	Road (L)
20.7	Road (L)
22.4	Corral on right. Ground is covered with blackbrush and yucca.
23.6	Road (L)
24.1	Cat Pasture

24.2 Early Weed Turnoff (L)
    4.8 — Road (L)
    5.3 — **TRAIL 25 — Fox Canyon**
        5.8 — **TRAIL 26 — Scorpion Gulch**
26.6 Dry Fork of Coyote Turnoff (L)
    0.6 — Take the left fork
    0.7 — Take the left fork
    1.7 — **TRAIL 27 — Dry Fork Coyote**
28.9 Cattleguard
29.6 Big Hollow Wash crossing
29.8 Road bed is purple
31.0 Road (L) to Liston Seep
31.5 Redwell Turnoff (L)
    1.2 — Take the left road
    1.5 — **TRAIL 28 — Redwell**
31.9 Cattleguard
33.8 King Mesa Jeep Road (L)
34.6 Cattleguard
34.7 **TRAIL 29 — Hurricane Wash**
    The road becomes quite curvy for the next two miles.
37.1 Fortymile Ridge road (L)
    5.0 — Take left fork
    7.0 — **TRAIL 30 — Fortymile Ridge**
37.8 **TRAIL 31 — Dance Hall Rock**
38.0 Cattleguard
38.5 Road to Fortymile Spring (L)
39.4 Good view of the country behind Dance Hall Rock as the road goes east for a brief while.
40.5 **TRAIL 32 — Fortymile Gulch Trailhead.** The actual drainage is Carcass Wash.
41.7 Sooner Wash
42.7 Turnoff to Willow Gulch (L)
    1.4 — **TRAIL 33 — Willow Gulch**
43.2 Cattleguard
44.7 Fiftymile Bench road (R)
45.6 The road crosses Willow Gulch
46.7 Cattleguard
46.9 **TRAIL 34 — Soda Gulch** (Fiftymile Creek). Cave Point and caves are visible toward the west.
48.6 Glen Canyon National Recreational Area boundary sign.
48.9 The Soda. This is the local name for Fiftymile Creek.
50.5 Soda Springs Cabin turnoff (R) — 0.2 of a mile to the cabin.
51.8 Cattleguard
52.0 **TRAIL 35 — Davis Gulch**
53.1 Hole-in-the-Rock Arch plaque (R). You can see the arch on the skyline to the west.
55.3 **TRAIL 36 — Clear Creek**
57.5 **TRAIL 37 — Hole-in-the-Rock.** This is the end of the road.

V. SUMMER HIKES

What to do when the canyon country is too hot, full of deer flies, and in danger of flooding? Go and explore where all of that water comes from. The Aquarius Plateau offers a delightful green contrast to the canyon color. The Forest Service has a number of campgrounds that can be used as a base camp, or there is the freedom to camp at large. If you are a fisherman, the many stocked lakes are another attraction. Since the plateau rises to well over 10,000 feet, moderate summer temperatures can be enjoyed. An array of flowers and small mammals attract the naturalist. The hikes listed are just a small sample of the recreational opportunities.

MILES	DESCRIPTION
0.0	Center of town — heading west
0.4	Forest Service Office on north side of street
0.8	BLM and NPS offices to the south
1.7	Turnoff to Petrified Forest State Park and Wide Hollow Reservoir.
5.0	Main Canyon Turnoff
	0.2 — North Canyon road turnoff (R). Take this road.
	7.7 — North Canyon Reservoir
	9.7 — White Flats road (R)
11.8	— Road (R)
12.6	— Road (R)
12.7	— Road crosses North Creek. This is a ford so take it slow and then give your brakes a chance to dry out. The area behind the sign has road closures. Vehicles are only allowed on the road to Lower and Upper Barker Reservoirs.
12.8	— Road (L)
13.1	— Road fords Twitchell Creek. The road climbs up the side of the hill away from North Canyon. There are lots of switchbacks.
16.1	— Area of aspen blowdowns
16.6	— Lower Barker Reservoir road (R)
17.2	— Barker Reservoir Campground
	TRAIL 38 — Barker Reservoir

TRAIL 39 — Posy Lake Lookout — See the Hell's Backbone Road Log.

TRAIL 40 — Jacob's Reservoir — See the Hell's Backbone Road Log.

TRAIL 41 — East Boulder Creek — See Highway 12 Road Log.

TRAIL 42a — Deer Creek Lake — See Highway 12 Road Log.

TRAIL 42b — Deer Creek Lake — See Highway 12 Road Log.

Pine Creek

TRAIL 1
PINE CREEK

Difficulty: Moderately Easy
Length (one way):   8 miles
Time: 1 Day
Maps: Posy Lake 7.5, Wide Hollow Reservoir 7.5
Water: Pine Creek

This is a delightful day stroll down a stream. The area known as The Box has high multi-colored sandstone walls, which contrast sharply with the dark green of the ponderosa pine trees. The route requires several stream crossings, but these are generally easy. There are pools for soaking, and broad sandy benches for camping. The canyons of Pine Creek and Death Hollow to the east were included in the recently passed Utah Wilderness Bill of 1984. The passage of this bill recognizes the outstanding wilderness qualities of these canyons.

Drive north out of Escalante, using the Hell's Backbone road log for mileage. The starting point is a small pullout at mile 18.8. The pullout is on the right hand side of the road next to a Forest Service sign that closes the area behind the sign to vehicles. If you are only going to take a short hike and explore the lower portion of Pine Creek, there is a small Forest Service sign eight miles north of Escalante directing you to the dirt road that goes to The Box.

From the pullout on the east side of the road, head straight down the hillside to creek level. In a quarter mile, cross back to the west side where Blue Spring Creek enters. A short walk up this stream will reward you with a view of a waterfall. Continuing down Pine Creek, the banks of the next mile are crowded with wild rose plants (Rosa woodsii). Careful route selection or long pants make travel through this section easier. The next challenge is a recent rockfall on the west bank. After you negotiate your way through the fallen trees, the walking becomes easier.

In another mile the canyon opens up on the east side and the sharp relief of the Navajo sandstone cliffs holds the eye. The red bark of the manzanita (Arctostaphylos pungens) shrubs contrasts majestically against the white sand. Geraniums, evening primroses, paintbrushes, skyrockets, and D.Y.C.'s dot the landscape. (A D.Y.C. is a darn yellow composite, part of the largest family of flowering plants and difficult to correctly identify.)

The sandy benches contain stands of tall ponderosa pine (Pinus ponderosa) trees, easily recognizable with their sets of three long needles. The scales of the bark of this tree resemble a bird or anything else you can imagine. It can grow to tremendous porportions, especially along the wetter Pacific Coast. The name ponderosa was suggested by David Douglass, the Scottish explorer of the Northwest. Valued for its timber, it is an integral part of the local economy. The seeds were eaten raw or made into bread by the Indians. Squirrels, chipmunks, and birds also enjoy the seeds.

After about another mile, Deep Creek comes in from the west. This creek can be used as a loop route if transportation hasn't been arranged at the mouth of The Box. This side drainage is well named because the banks are steep. It is easier to walk on the north hillside above the stream. There is a delicate waterfall in this drainage.

The red stalk with the cluster of whitish bell-like flowers found near the mouth of Deep Creek is a species which cannot manufacture its own food. Woodland pinedrops (Pterospora andromedea), part of the Heather family, utilizes the food made by the fungi that decay fallen plant material.

Heading down canyon, the next half-mile is more intimate. The path is closer to the stream and the sandstone walls crowd the creek bank. When side drainages appear on the east side, The Box opens up and presents a display of crossbedded, multi-tiered, sandstone walls. After the next stream crossing, the path remains on the east bank for awhile. In most places there is a passageway on either bank and you can choose the number of stream crossings. There are three types of crossings: walking across fallen tree trunks, boulder hopping, or wading.

At the first large promontory on the east bank that forces the stream to bend, the path follows the streambed. At the next outcropping, the route goes over the back side of the sandstone wedge. The sandy benches provide ample campsites. The final mile is twisty as the stream turns southwest and cuts its way through the Escalante Monocline. There is a fence in one of the constricted bends, then one or two more water crossings and you're out of The Box.

TRAIL 2
DEATH HOLLOW

Difficulty: Extremely strenuous
Length (one way): 22.5 miles
Time: 4 Days
Maps: Roger Peak 7.5, Escalante 7.5
Water: Middle Death Hollow

*This is the most difficult and challenging hike described in this book.
The beautiful canyon is the epitome of contrasts. There is no water for the
first eleven miles and then you are constantly swimming for the next three
miles. The section near the telephone line is fairly easy, but there is thick
vegetation. Near the mouth of Mamie Creek, another potential swim
through more narrows is another challenge. Poison ivy is found in the lower
portion.*

*Before you start on this adventure, make sure that you are physically
and mentally prepared. Protect your gear in the best waterproof containers
you have. Bring emergency warm clothes to offset potential hypothermia.
Take some parachute cord to lower packs. Take a tall friend that is
proficient in stemming and chimneying techniques. A one-person inflatable
boat would be a great help. Make sure of the weather before you go.
Threatening storms could produce flash floods.*

There is no clearly marked trailhead for this hike. Use the Hell's
Backbone road log as a starter. Pull off the side of the road when the white
cliff is visible through the trees to the north. The descent is a gradual slope.
Once you are on the floor of the drainage, the walk is a gentle stroll down a
sandy wash. Towering Navajo cross-striated sandstone cliffs form the
backdrop. Tall ponderosa pine trees add green and yellow hues.

After four miles or so an eastern arm runs closely parallel. There is
only a small rise separating the two drainages. The canyon narrows after
awhile, but the same motif of sandy floor and white walls continue. This
general impression of white is what remains in the memory of this upper
section.

The variability of conditions at different times of the year and the
effects of recent flash floods all influence the situation which will appear
next. The winter of 1983 was extremely dry, so early spring trips the
following year were easy but dry. The pools were filled with sand and areas
that normally require swimming were easily negotiated. Several years ago,
all the pools were scoured out and full of water, requiring tremendous
effort to negotiate.

It is possible to walk on the sandstone edge around the first several
pools created by chockstones blocking the streambed, but the walls quickly
became too steep and a central route through the pools becomes necessary.

Death Hollow

Some of the barrier stones are easy to scramble over, while others require a jump into the water below.

The last several pools were covered with floating debris and again we found a way around them.

When the chockstones and pools end, you are able to take the time to look around and appreciate the dynamic quality of the surrounding sandstone. As the stream mellows the small waterfalls, contrasting white and black patterns on the walls, and the increased green streamside vegetation all come together for a better feeling of what this canyon has to offer.

Note the spurter spring gushing several inches out of the ground on the south side. The vegetation makes it a challenge to cross from one side of the stream to the other. When the canyon continues in an easterly direction for awhile, look for the telephone line spanned across the canyon. The large cave on the northern wall is another indicator. This is where the Boulder Mail Trail comes down from Slickrock Saddle Bench.

Although there are numerous stream crossings in the next three miles, continued use has worn a path along the sandy benches. Several perpendicular narrow slots take off on the east wall. The large bench and rocky western wall is part of the original Boulder Mail route. Rockfalls that made horse travel impossible ended travel out of Death Hollow at this point.

Around the bend the canyon narrows again. The lake that had been created behind the rockslide has been washed away. We built a raft of washed down logs to ferry our packs across this artificial lake. The next section of narrows contains lots of ledges, so it might be possible to skirt some of the deeper pools.

Now there are some serious bends in the stream as the canyon works its way around some large, protruding blocks of sandstone. Walking is easy from here on out, either on sandy banks next to the stream or on the shallow bedrock.

There's a tremendous overhang cut under the dry waterfall coming in high on the western wall. Poison ivy (Rhus radicans) is much in evidence in the greenery below the overhang. Another mile of sand and bedrock walking in the stream and you will reach the junction with the Escalante River. If you turn upstream at this point, it is 7.5 miles up the Escalante River to the road by the cemetery. (See TRAIL 5 for a description of this section.) If you head downstream, it's 7.4 miles to Highway 12.

Sand Creek wall stain

TRAIL 3
SAND CREEK

Difficulty: Strenuous
Length (one way):   20.5 miles
Time: 3 to 4 Days
Maps: Roger Peak 7.5, Escalante 7.5, Calf Creek 7.5
Water: Sand Creek

This generally narrow canyon offers an adventure for well-prepared backpackers. Starting as a mountain stream that drains part of the Aquarius Plateau, it winds its way through slickrock benches to the Escalante River. The name was derived from those sandy formations, but it is often an apt description of the water. Brush and boulders make progress difficult. Solitude and exemplary scenery make this trip well worth the effort.

Follow the Hell's Backbone road northeast out of Escalante for 28.3 miles to the Forest Service sign for Sand Creek. Start down the stream where it crosses the road. There is plenty of room to pull off the road on the east side of Sand Creek. Fendler rose (Rosa fendleri) and its stickers greet you right away. The fruits of this plant are the edible and highly nutritious rose hips, containing large amounts of vitamin A and C. They also provide food for a variety of animals and birds. Concentrated patches present a hindrance to travel.

In the first half-mile, Grimes Creek and an unnamed little tributary add their flows to Sand Creek. When the walls start to close in, it's easier to traverse the sandy slopes above the creek. The banks become quite steep.

There are innumerable small waterfalls along the way, varying from one to two feet high. They are caused by boulders blocking the stream or trees that have fallen across. The channel remains very narrow, and when there are sandy benches, they are covered by manzanita and wild rose bushes. A recent flash flood had uprooted many trees and further blocked the passage, making this first part of the trip a serious endurance test.

There is a rapid drop in elevation as this stream steadily cuts down through the sandstone cliffs. Having left the blue spruce (Picea pungens) trees behind near the trailhead, ponderosa pine and Douglas-fir (Psuedotsuga menziesii) cover the sandy slopes. The Douglas-fir cone is distinctive because it has "mouse-tails" sticking out from between the cone scales. It is not a true fir, because its cones fall off whole and they hang down. A coffee substitute used to be made from the needles and twigs. The state tree of Oregon, it is a valuable lumber tree in the northwest.

The first western tributary is a narrow slit in the sandstone, ending quickly in a twenty foot dry waterfall. The narrow channel continues to wind its way southeast. Rocky Mountain Juniper (Juniperus scopolorum)

Sand Creek sandstone striations

and red-osier dogwood (Cornus stolonifera) are found at streamside. The bright red bark makes this an easy plant to identify. The pliable stems resemble the osier (willow) and were used in making baskets.

The first really good spots to camp occur when the canyon widens around the entrance of the first eastern tributary. It takes five hours to get to this point. The canyon quickly narrows again after this bend. The convoluted passage is broken by a series of narrow openings to the west. They don't go far before they pinch out.

All of a sudden an opening appears in the skyline and the high sandstone walls recede. You enter into a broad open valley with cottonwood (Populus fremontii) trees along the stream and Utah juniper (Juniperus osteosperma) on the sloping hillsides. Campsites are plentiful. For the next two miles there are cattle paths on the benchland that can be followed. The rock layers are mudstones and shales that range from white to pinkish red. The banks are lined with willow shoots and beaver (Castor canadensis) tracks.

Going on, the Navajo sandstone appears again and the canyon narrows but there is still plenty of walking room. Right after the western side slot, you pass a small grove of Gambel oak (Quercus gambelii) and several scooped out pools as the creek cuts through bedrock. The benches are covered with golden rabbitbrush (Chrysothamnus nauseosus). The light grayish green stalks of this tall bush are an aid in identification.

When the canyon opens up again there is a display of sandstone pillars and balancing rocks. There is an easy route on the eastern bank. The mouth

Boynton road

of the next western tributary is barely discernable because of the heavy plant growth at its mouth.

A half-mile or so before Sweetwater Creek enters, the Boynton Road crosses Sand Creek. This road was built to give easier access between Escalante and the scattered ranches in Salt Gulch. Very little evidence of this early 1900s road is left, since heavy rains washed out portions shortly after it was built.

The indication that Sweetwater Creek is close by occurs when a walkable ledge appears on the west bank. When this terrace slopes down, cross the stream and continue the journey on the eastern ledge.

At the dry hollow entering from the east, several large volcanic rock cairns should be visible. These mark the Boulder Mail Trail, used to carry mail between Escalante and Boulder in the early 1900s.

It's time to thrash through the willows again. The large boulders in the stream make for slippery, treacherous crossings. There are several long, constricted areas where wading or swimming is required. In one pool, the water came right to my chin. It's tricky to negotiate those narrows because the silt gets stirred up so it's impossible to see the slippery sloping walls under water.

The streamside vegetation crowds in again when there is room to walk on the banks. The tall plants with the cluster of purple flowers is common milkweed (Asclepias speciosa). The stems become fibrous as they get older, and yield a strong fiber that the Indians used for cordage.

The canyon country is in a constant state of flux. One year there are serious rockfalls, another year they are washed away. So a pool that had formed behind the rockfall is gone. The narrow eastern side slot has a water seep. One small-flowered columbine (Aquilegia micrantha) was growing near the seep. A deep violet and yellow color made this flower very conspicuous.

The canyon is easier to negotiate a mile or so above Willow Patch Creek, with deepening walls replacing the heavy brush. There is a stand of oak trees that makes for a scenic campspot on the high northern sand bench where the canyon really widens. Sagebrush (Artemesia tridentata) covers the wide, flat benchland.

A wandering garter snake (Thamnophis elegans vagrans) was spotted along the stream. This fast, non-poisonous snake has a distinct dorsal stripe and separate dark blotches. For the next mile, willow thickets crowd the stream and progress is slow.

Sand Hollow forms a dry waterfall just before it joins Sand Creek. The walking becomes easier as there is a path to follow and the vegetation is not as thick. The walls are high above as the stream winds along the last two miles. There is a spring at the wide sandy mouth of Sand Creek.

Three miles of travel down the Escalante River brings you to the junction with Calf Creek and Highway 12 (TRAIL 5).

Tinaja

Boulder airport

TRAIL 4
BOULDER MAIL TRAIL

Difficulty: Strenuous
Length (one way):   16 Miles
Time: 2 to 3 Days
Maps: Boulder Town 7.5, Calf Creek 7.5, Escalante 7.5
Water: Sand Creek and Death Hollow. Seasonally water
pockets may be found in Mamie Creek and on Antone
Flat.

This is an exciting route for experienced backpackers who are capable of orienteering across broken country and in and out of several steep drainages. There are expansive vistas, outstanding opportunities for untrammeled wilderness exploration, and challenging slickrock hiking. The route is an important part of the early history of Escalante and Boulder.

The small dirt road that heads south off the Hell's Backbone road, .2 of a mile before it rejoins Highway 12, is the start of the Boulder Mail Trail. The easiest way to get there is to drive 24.8 miles east of Escalante on Highway 12, and then turn left on the Hell's Backbone road (to Salt Gulch). Take the first dirt road to the left. (You can drive this jeep road until the trail diverges in a couple of miles but there are no good places to park at that junction.)

There's a place to park on the left among the junipers after you've pulled off the Hell's Backbone road. Walk down the jeep road that crosses the Boulder airstrip. Note the tower marking the airstrip. As this road starts heading down you can see the mesa of McGath Point Bench in the distance to the south. After you pass a very wide and tall pinyon pine tree (a great shade stop), start looking on the right side for the yellow flagging. This marks the junction with a dirt track that takes off in a southwesterly direction. To make the route more obvious, blaze marks have been cut into the trees. Eventually the flagging will be removed. Follow these until you come to exposed sandstone, making sure to follow the blazes. The route turns away from the dirt tracks. Cairns mark the descent. The route is flagged through the sagebrush until you break into bare country again. Then descend down this cairned draw. When you look down the sandstone there appears to be a big fissure crack in front of you; the rock cairns lead you to the left and around it. This drainage takes you down to Sand Creek.

Cross the creek on the dark volcanic boulders that make convenient stepping stones. Then walk downstream along the west bank of the creek, finding a way through the willows. When the stream crowds against the western wall, a cairn marks the spot to head up the hillside. Contour around the hill, following the path that leads you to the dry drainage

Boulder mail trail

coming in on the right. Cross this draw and continue south until you hit a cairn indicating the point to climb out of Sand Creek. This shallow depression does not qualify as a draw or side drainage.

Starting in 1902, this route was traveled on a bi-weekly basis by postal riders. Before this time, mail delivery to Boulder had been sporadic. Mules were used to carry packages and supplies. In 1924, cans of cream also were shipped by this method, destined for the creamery at Osiris. This was the preferred summer route because it was about 10 miles shorter than the Boulder road, which Utah 12 generally follows.

As you are struggling up the slickrock, you can see a butte on the horizon. The route heads around the right side of this butte. The cairned way heads up on the back side of this butte. The dry drainage you recently crossed is visible below you. Continue on the flagged route in a southwesterly direction toward a break in the Slickrock Saddle Bench. Spectacular views of Boulder Mountain, the Henry Mountains, and McGath Point are visible to the east. A portion of the old telephone line is present on your right and it can be used as a guideline across the slickrock.

If you follow the telephone line, it will lead you to a precipitous view of Death Hollow. The cairned route down follows a steep side draw slightly to the south. Go down the draw until it pinches out. Then the cairns take you northwest along the crack. Evidence remains of portions of the old trail that have been blasted out of the rock. Just before you drop to creek level, there is a huge alcove on the right. The trail continues to zigzag down the slickrock to the creek bed.

As you head down canyon, look up and see the telephone line passing overhead. This line is part of the old Forest Service telephone system, established in 1910. It serviced thirty-five families in the Boulder area. Reeves Baker, a long time Escalante resident, interviewed by Rex Welles of the BLM, had the following comments to make about the system:

Well, if you wanted me they'd ring two short ones and a long one. If they wanted my neighbor they'd ring maybe two long ones and a short, but everyone had his individual ring, and if you wanted to talk to your neighbor you had to know what his ring was, you just ring it, whatever his ring was, that was the way they did, and then if they wanted to talk over here [Escalante], they'd call Shurtz and he had a switchboard there where he'd connect you with the family you wanted in Escalante, or anywhere as far as that goes. It was quite a phone line too. It was made up of bailing wire and small scraps of barbed wire. If you wanted to fix the line and you didn't have any phone wire you'd pick up a piece of barbed wire and put it in the gap. It was just a patched up affair.

The descent into Death Hollow is a steep seven hundred foot drop. It was named because a pack animal fell to its death into the gorge. There is lots of box elder (Acer negundo) growing along the stream. The brown, dried up leaves cling to your clothing when you pass by.

Mamie Natural Bridge

After six bends going downstream, or about a half-mile, you'll come to a bend going to the right. There is a lone tall dead ponderosa pine trunk on the right bank. Turn west and look for the cairn at eye level. If you start to pass a narrow side slot coming in from the east, backtrack a sixteenth of a mile. The cairned route takes you up the slickrock. When the juniper trees appear, the yellow and white flagging leads you around the west end of that north-facing escarpment.

Where the flagging ends at the top of the ridge, head southeast until the telephone line is encountered. Follow the line in a southwesterly direction across the plateau. This section of the mail route came into use when rockslides made the other route out of Death hollow impassable for horses. The original route went about three miles further along the creekbed before climbing out. This newer route is shorter and easier than the old climb.

Leaving the sagebrush and junipers, cairns are used again to mark the route through the open sandstone country. Just before the drop into Mamie Creek, the way descends to the right of the point straight ahead. Once in the sandy wash, go downstream about 80 yards to the rim of the first plunge pool. A cairn and white flagging up the hill to the right lead you up and out of the wash. When you've located the route out, put down your pack and take a short side hike.

A mile walk down the wash will bring you to one of those secret delights of canyon exploration. Not marked on the topographic map is a thirty foot high natural bridge that surprises you shortly after rounding a sharp bend. This is followed by an abrupt pouroff. There is an urge in canyon country to go just one more bend and in this case the reward is a grand display.

The climb out of Mamie Creek is in a southwesterly direction, skirting both rock promontories on the right. The route follows the old telephone line for a brief period, but the wire ends abruptly. In the open country of Antone Flat, the flagging is on dead standing junipers. There are deep natural tanks in the next drainage. Cairns take you west and up the wash, and then skirt south along the base of the ridge. This section has about eighty cairns to mark the route. Angling west along another section of the telephone line, you can see the scrape marks left by the horses where they were persuaded to make a three foot jump up.

The route stays high around this side drainage of Pine Creek and heads over the top of the last hill. The big "E" that has been whitewashed into the hillside stands for "Escalante." A well-worn zigzag path brings you down to Pine Creek. The land along the creek is private land so it is advisable to stay on the east bank of Pine Creek and follow it south until it joins the Escalante River. Go west upriver until it opens up. Then turn south up the shallow draw and through the sage flats until you hit the dirt road east of the cemetery. Follow this road west and it will take you to Highway 12.

There are two places to leave a car if you have a shuttle organized. This road continues a short distance past the western edge of the dump. That is one spot. The other is just east of the cemetery next to the fence, once you are past the cattleguard. Where this dirt road leaves Highway 12, you are a little over a mile from the town of Escalante.

Arch on Escalante River

TRAIL 5
ESCALANTE RIVER—
TOWN TO CALF CREEK

Difficulty: Easy
Length (one way):   14.9 miles
Time: 2 Days
Maps: Escalante 7.5, Calf Creek 7.5
Water: Escalante River, Death Hollow, Sand Creek

This is the easiest part of the river to hike. Usually the flow is only ankle deep. There are places to camp along the whole stretch. Impressive cliffs of multi-colored, fissured, striated, and textured sandstone line the channel. A skyline arch and natural bridge are interesting geological features as well as photographic challenges.

Going east on highway 12 out of Escalante, turn left in just over a mile. The cemetery is highly visible when you enter this dirt road. Cross the cattleguard and head east.

Stay on the road past the cemetery until just past the west edge of the town dump. Head down the hill to the north until you come to the fence. The best place to cross the fence is where it straddles the wash. Avoid the luxuriant growth of tamarisk (Tamarix pentandra) or salt cedar at the mouth of the wash. This finely branched shrub, bearing clusters of showy pink flowers in the spring and summer, creates a nightmare obstacle for hikers. Thick stands will be encountered further down the river, leaving indelible marks on your body. Skirt these shrubby trees on either side. Suddenly you're at the river.

The tilted edge of the Escalante Monocline is an imposing mass of sandstone rock. The narrow channel that the river has cut through these massive, white domes is a gateway to another world.

Almost immediately Pine Creek enters from the north, substantially adding to the volume of the river. That conical structure is the gauging station. The banks are dotted with boulders of various hues that were deposited by previous flash floods. The surrounding cliffs have cracks running in every conceivable direction. The colors of the rock vary from pure white, to rust, to dark brown. The black desert varnish streaks add another tone.

After an hour of walking through this sinuous portion of the canyon, you come around a bend with a low dividing ridge. The whole north wall is a sheltered overhang; a bowl scooped out of the cliff. This is one of the largest overhangs in the canyon.

Both sides of the canyon have narrow slots that drop precipitously into

the main canyon. There is one on the north side that makes a sharp turn away from the river and leaves a tall bench of sandstone as foreground scenery. The backdrop is a long vertical black streak that pours over the far cliff wall.

The canyon straightens somewhat a mile before the junction with Mamie Creek. Streamside vegetation starts to appear. Before this the only green was on the benchland away from the river. A series of rock ledge outcroppings appear next to the bank. The rust streaked patterned ledges have had small pockets scooped out. These have filled with small pebbles, creating miniature rock gardens. One of the drainage patterns that comes from Antone Flat enters the Escalante in a spectacular, narrow "V" high above the river.

Death Hollow enters from the north in less than a half-mile. This lively stream cascades over sandstone layers. A short hike up this challenging canyon will bring you to several carved out swimming holes. There is poison ivy along the path a half-mile up. (The three oaklike leaves are the warning sign to avoid this plant.)

By now you have passed the common trees found along a riparian habitat: willow, tamarisk, box elder, and that large, stately, shade provider, the Fremont cottonwood. This tree is found near a water source, since it is not specifically adapted to a desert climate. It was first described by John Charles Fremont, a man who certainly made his mark on western history.

What looks like a snowstorm in spring is the blowing white male catkins from the cottonwood tree. The inner bark of this tree is palatable to horses, so Fremont referred to it as sweet cottonwood. The branches are in competition with each other, so there is a constant self-pruning going on in the crown.

66

There are shallow caves against the walls in this next section before Sand Creek. It is an easy passage from one sand bar to another. When there is a serious openness to the canyon, Sand Creek is not far away.

On the north shore, just before the stream hits the wall at the last bend before Sand Creek, a dugway has been cut going up the hill. This is a remnant of the Boynton Road, built in 1909 to serve as a shortcut between Escalante and the ranches at Salt Gulch.

A large level sandy area is found right at the mouth of Sand Creek. A seep is found near the mouth that provides clearer water than is usually gotten from the river. Deep pools are found a short way up this convoluted canyon.

Around the first bend of the Escalante, a huge hole is evident on the skyline. The patterns on the wall that frame this arch make this one of the most striking arches found in this canyon country. Another bend reveals Escalante Natural Bridge. A natural bridge is created by running water erosion, while an arch is formed by weathering of stressed areas of rock until a hole is formed.

The rest of the stroll to Highway 12 is along a well-worn path. A historical site that has faded with time is Phipp's grave. His boots had marked the grave. In 1878, John Boynton and his partner, Washington Phipps, had a falling out. Phipps was shot.

Stay on the south side as you approach the bridge. There is a gate in the fence along the wall and this route respects property rights on the other bank.

Screech owl

Maverick drainage into Phipps Canyon

Phipps Arch

TRAIL 6
PHIPPS WASH

Difficulty: Strenuous
Length (one way):   5.5 miles
Time: 1 Day
Maps: Tenmile Flat 7.5, Calf Creek 7.5
Water: Bring your own; there is only seasonal water in Phipps

This is a premium day hike, with a forty foot high arch and a natural bridge as two of the outstanding features. A colorful canyon, which usually has some water flowing near the lower end, combines challenging, slickrock hiking with an easy stroll along a willow streambed. A loop trip can be made by hiking a mile up the Escalante River to Highway 12.

Follow the Highway 12 road log east of Escalante for 10.9 miles. Just before the road turns sharply to the left, marked with a black and yellow arrow highway sign, turn right onto the dirt road. There is a shallow pullout on the right in .3 mile.

The most challenging part of the hike is this first slickrock descent to a

Maverick Natural Bridge

side wash that drains into Phipps. (If this route looks too exciting for you, the road log notes a place to pull off on Highway 12. This dry side fork is an easy half-mile walk and brings you to the same wash as described here.)

The road you're on is named after Sam Sheffield, an early settler who homesteaded on the Escalante River in the early 1890s. The road travels through deep sand until it reaches the rim of the Escalante river canyon, where Sheffield reportedly constructed a short log causeway to get down to a sand dune. He stayed at his farm on the river for only a few years, resettling in Boulder, where he died in 1916. The chimney is all that is left of his homestead.

The route starts due east of your car. There is an obvious V in the domes. Head down the slickrock of this shallow opening. When it rims out, a stairstep slickrock descent angling to the south brings you to the sand. A dark red wall just past where you drop down is an easy landmark for the return trip.

You're free to roam in a northerly direction on any route you select. The area known as "Head-of-the-Rocks" is visible as a swirling white domed slickrock mass to your left. In less than a half-mile you should intersect the shallow side draw. If you hit it where a short dry arm descends from the highway, there should be a pool at the junction.

The wash heads in an easterly direction, and is easy sand hiking. When it takes an abrupt turn to the south, it is time to leave the wash. A dry water fall stops that part of the hike. Staying on the west side, a sand dune provides easy access to the base of the waterfall. There may be a large pool of water just below this fluted jump.

Crossing the fence, a short sandy walk brings you to the junction with the main Phipps Wash. The high walls are adorned with photogenic displays of desert varnish. When the wash heads north, a short eastern opening ends in a rincon, or hollowed area.

Heading north, water appears at ground level. Although there is still plenty of sand, the green vegetation changes the complexion of the wash.

The route up to Phipps Arch starts on the north side of the mouth of the short, eastern box canyon. Contour east and then up the ledges and slickrock. This scramble requires the use of hands in several spots. Be aware of loose rocks. The route angles northeast until it hits one of several very shallow sandstone drainages.

This upper level has large pocketed sandstone domes. One of these has worn through as Phipps Arch. This majestic rock is bright orange, painted with dark streaks of desert varnish.

While I was climbing around northwest of the arch, my hat blew off into an enclosed sandy basin. Since the walls were too steep to climb, we returned with a climbing rope. Tying off at the base of a bush, I lowered myself down what appeared to be a straight drop. Imagine my surprise when the last six feet were undercut. This small basin ended in a sheer two hundred foot drop. Inspired by my lack of choice, I pulled myself and my hat back up the rope.

Sculptured water pockets and an overhanging alcove are found at the end of the box canyon just south of the arch. The main canyon has also scooped out water pockets in the red bedrock. Luxurious growth lines the bank. In the fall, the conspicuous fluffy white balls of the western virgin's bower (Clemantis ligusticifolia) cover the bushes. This vine clings to whatever is available. The plant was chewed by Indians and settlers as a sore throat and cold remedy.

The western drainage heads to Maverick Natural Bridge. There is a trail on the southern side that gets you out of the streambed so you can walk on top of this fin and further up canyon. It deadends in a dry waterfall in a half-mile. This tributary used to be fenced at its mouth and held weaned calves.

Another mile down Phipps will bring you to the cottonwood-covered wide mouth. This wash is named after Washington Phipps, who kept a herd of horses in the area. He was a partner with John Boynton, who lived a mile up the river. The partners had a falling out. Phipps threatened his former partner and was shot. His grave used to be visible upstream from Calf Creek. Boynton gave himself up, was not indicted, sold his stock and left the area.

If you do not want to retrace your steps back up the wash, it is less than a mile up the Escalante River to Highway 12.

TRAIL 7
ESCALANTE RIVER—
CALF CREEK TO
HARRIS WASH

Difficulty: Moderately strenuous
Length (one way): 26.4 miles
Time: 3 to 4 Days
Maps: Calf Creek 7.5, King Bench 7.5, Red Breaks 7.5
Water: Escalante River, Boulder Creek, The Gulch, Harris Wash

This varied section is full of wonderful surprises. Areas with wide benches alternate with closed-in vertical walls. Side canyon exploration alone can easily double the time spent here. The ruin of a homestead settled in the 1890s adds historical flavor. Below Horse Canyon the walking becomes much easier. Exiting out Harris Wash brings you to the Hole-in-the-Rock road and a relatively easy loop connection.

Go approximately fifteen miles east of Escalante on Highway 12 to where the highway crosses the river. There are places to park next to the BLM sign. Of interest here is the Moqui house on the north bank across from the sign. At the trailhead be aware that both banks of the river downstream are private property. The trail starts on the south side behind the trail register. There is a sign indicating the place to cross the river to the north side. (Besides, you want to avoid Mr. Bowman's large and noisy dogs.)

After the second river crossing you're back on the south side. The fence marks the boundary of the Escalante Canyons Outstanding Natural Area. It was the colorful description of this area in a BLM publication that first enticed me into exploring this area. The canyon already has two layers, the Kayenta ledges of reddish, purple rock found near stream level and the domed cap rock of Navajo sandstone.

Phipps Wash (Trail 6) is the first southern tributary. The mouth has a wide sandy entrance, but the flowing water and the rapidly enclosing walls give this side canyon its enchantment. Cottonwood trees cover the sandy mouth, with an occasional dark red barked tree found at streamside. This tree is Russian-olive (Elaeagnus angustifolia), which is also easily recognized by the silvery colored leaves and fruit. Introduced from Russia as windbreaks and an ornamental shade tree, it has spread widely along streams. It emits a fragrant odor from its small yellow flowers.

Another short side canyon comes in from the north in another mile.

Bowington Arch

Known locally as Deer Canyon because of the profusion of mule deer found there, a short hike up this canyon leads to Boynton (Bowington) Arch. You have to bypass three small plunge pools on the way upstream. A multi-colored display of boulders covers the bed of Deer Canyon between the first two pools. A short climb around the western side takes you above the third pool.

When the canyon splits, the main fork goes to the right. Bear left and the arch is visible high up in the next left spur. A scramble through the oak trees and up the sandy slope brings you almost underneath the protruding fin that contains the arch.

The main canyon remains fairly wide through here. The hardest part of the stream crossings is the slippery vegetation that grows right on the steep banks. A couple of miles above the mouth of Boulder Creek, the layered Kayenta goes underground. With only the Navajo present, the walls start to close in.

It's easy to miss the mouth of Boulder Creek, because it is well hidden by willow and tamarisk thickets. There is usually a strong flow of water coming down this canyon. Even a short side trip up Boulder Creek (Trail 9) reveals the scenic splendor of this very pretty canyon.

Around the next bend a fence stretches clear across the river. The gate is on the south end against the wall. Now the willow thickets crowd the bank and make it difficult to locate and negotiate a route. The whiplash action of the willows is a serious obstacle to avoid. Often the route hugs the walls on the inside of the bend. Sometimes it is easier to walk down the middle of the

Escalante River

Side slot

Transverse crack

Author in water pocket

Willow thickets

Side drainage narrows

stream. Several large sandstone blocks have separated from the wall, creating a visual discontinuity to the straight smooth walls.

Two bends after the rockfall there is a fine campsite located on the west bank. Several more twists and a narrow crack appears on the west wall. There is no route up this, but there is a deep pool at its mouth. The cave to the north invites exploration. From here to The Gulch the canyon widens. Where the stream flows over sandstone ripples, a ledge rapid occurs in low water. The canyon appears more broken because of the perpendicular cracks running away from the stream.

When you come to the wide bend where the river doubles back on itself, there is a route out using the slot coming in from the southwest. The bend has several good campsites. This side trip is exciting, dangerous, strenuous, and geologically very interesting. With two tough scrambles, a way can be made to the slickrock expanses above the canyon.

(Cross the river and head up the side stream. It ends very quickly at a pool and an impassable chute. Walk up the sand hill covered with box elder. This tree is really a maple, although the toothed leaflets are very un-maple-like. When yellow, these leaves readily stick to your clothing. The double-winged seeds are airborne.

Go up the rockslide in the slot furthest to the right. Carefully pick your way up until you peak out on the domed slickrock above. Head south until you can drop back down to the level of the wash. A look down the wash to where it disappears into a dark slot brings you full circle to the narrow fissure you looked at from below.

Heading up the wash, a series of plunge pools require a detour on either side. Past these narrows, the drainage opens into a wide sandy wash. A small natural bridge has been carved out of the bedrock. The striking red flowers of the hedgehog cactus (Echinocereus triglochidiatus), or claret cup, is found along this wash. These plants have adapted to the desert by storing water in their stems. This green part of the cactus also manufactures food through the photosynthetic process. Leaves have been modified to sharp spines.

Another half mile brings you to a series of cracks that take off perpendicular to the main wash. These are a series of tensional joints, caused by vertical uplift in the area. They are different from faults because there has been no vertical displacement.

The first slot to the right goes for almost a mile before a pool blocks further dry progress. The main wash deadends in two dry waterfalls. Continuing past the first branches, the second crack on the right is a dangerous scramble route out to the slickrock above. The silverbush or round leaf buffaloberry (Shepherdia rotundifolia) that blocks the passage just before the rim needs to be carefully circumvented. Make double sure of your handholds in this chimney. The buffaloberry is an evergreen shrub with silvery coated, rounded leaves. It is the only native representative of the Oleaster family.)

Another mile of walking down the widening Escalante River brings you to the mouth of The Gulch (Trail 13). Although there is still heavy streamside vegetation, the insides of each bend are more open and passable.

Beaver cuttings

The first southern bend past The Gulch has a spring where water gushes from the wall. On the north shore there is a nice beach for camping.

The river has increased in velocity in the mile or so past The Gulch. The vertical walls are offset by talus slopes at the lower part. Beaver sign is common where they have gnawed through young cottonwood trees. There are several meanders where the river almost doubles back on itself. Just before Horse Canyon, an abandoned, entrenched meander or rincon is found on the north side.

The wide mouth of Horse Canyon (Trail 14) is also passed on the north side. Around the bend a skyline arch can be seen. From Horse to Harris the sandy benches make for an easy walk. The main struggle is finding a way through the stream-edge thickets. Once through, there is usually a well defined path on the inside of each bend.

Isolated sandstone monoliths and sand slopes capture the eye to the west. Going up the last sand dune and up the eight foot wall at the rim will connect you with the old Sheffield road. Two more bends and the chimney in the large open area of Sheffield Bend is all that is left of the old homestead. After Sam Sheffield moved to Boulder, the site was lived on by a bootlegger named Bill Isabell. He remained a year or so and then also moved to Boulder.

The marshy area just west of the chimney was Sam Sheffield's water source. The mosquitoes were so thick one spring that we had to camp on the opposite shore. Following the stream up the more southerly of the alcoves visible behind the chimney leads back to a quiet amphitheater, an idyllic rest spot.

Continuing downstream, the course of the river is quite convoluted and most of your time is spent crossing the benches from one meander to the next. There may be a small amount of surface water in the first drainage coming from Big Bown Bench about a quarter mile up canyon.

The next tributary from the north has a cattle trail crossing one jump above the mouth. Starting by the gate around the corner from the mouth, it climbs steeply to the rim of Big Bown Bench.

Due south across the river is a huge sand slide. This can be used as an exit route. Several miles of westerly cross country travel brings you to a jeep road that ends up at the Harris trailhead.

Several more bends and Silver Falls Creek becomes visible. The next fence has a gate on the south side of the river. If you stay on the west bank across from Silver Falls, Harris Wash (Trail 19) comes in obliquely from the northwest.

You can exit the river out Silver Falls Creek (Trail 17) to the east or out Harris Wash to the west. If you want to continue downstream, the rest of the river route description is found in Trail 21.

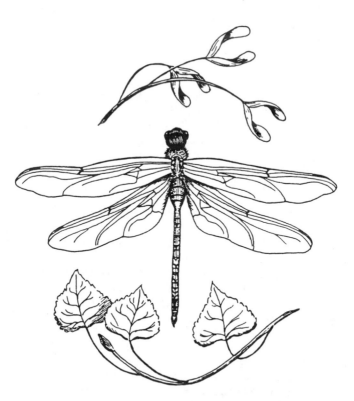

Wall stains on Escalante River

Lower Calf Creek Falls

TRAIL 8
LOWER CALF
CREEK FALLS

Difficulty: Moderate
Length (one way):   2¾ miles
Time: 3 Hours
Maps: Calf Creek 7.5
Water: Bring your own

This sandy hike is on a self-guided nature trail along Calf Creek. Petroglyphs, Indian ruins, and a beautiful canyon are all part of this pleasant walk. The falls and surrounding shady pool make this an absolutely necessary trip for anyone visiting the area.

Follow the Highway 12 road log. There is a large sign indicating the turn to the BLM campground down by Calf Creek. Park by the picnic area on the right and walk down the road.

The trail starts at the sign in the campground just before the road crosses the creek. There is a box with trail pamphlets that provide interpretation for the numbered stakes along the way. This information brochure translates the things you see so that you can have a better understanding of your surroundings.

The campground was built in 1963 with the trail to the falls completed in 1969. There are several places where the trail has been rerouted so it's important to watch for trail closures. The time of year can affect the difficulty of the hike because most of the trail is exposed to the sun. The sandy path also adds to the difficulty of the walk. Several benches are provided as rest spots.

The stream became known as Calf Creek because pioneer stockmen used this box canyon as a natural corral where calves were weaned. The shrill cries of a belted kingfisher (Megaceryle alcyon) can occasionally be heard as you intrude upon his fishing flights. This bird utilizes the telephone line as a perch from which to swoop along the shallow stream. The lush riparian habitat provides ample cover for a large variety of other birds.

A delightful swimming hole and a hundred and twenty-six foot falls are found at the end of the trail. The water can be surprisingly cool and this is certainly one of the premium spots found in the canyons of the Escalante area.

TRAIL 9
DRY HOLLOW—
BOULDER CREEK

Difficulty: Moderately Strenuous
Length (one way):   8 miles
Time: 1 Day
Maps: Calf Creek 7.5, King Bench 7.5
Water: Boulder Creek

This is an exciting hike that combines slickrock walking, struggling through thick streamside vegetation, stream wading, and some swimming. The photographic potentials are excellent, ranging from the large scale views of sandstone domes to intricate streamside patterns. This trip is for experienced and adventuresome backpackers who are looking for an infrequently traveled route. The challenges of this hike are an integral part of the wilderness experience found in hiking the Escalante canyons. Except for the short section of narrows, there are numerous places to camp along the way.

Take Highway 12 east of Escalante for 19.6 miles. The road has just finished climbing to the top of Haymaker Bench. A small sandy pullout on the right is the starting point, just before milemarker 79. There is a telephone pole on top of the rise right where you pull off the highway.

From the pullout on the east side of Highway 12, head east down the hill. The first thirty feet or so are the most difficult as the ground is overlain with volcanic debris. Head in a southeasterly direction toward the notch where Dry Hollow joins Boulder Creek.

As you are heading down the hillside, you will cross part of the old historic Boulder road. Access to Boulder has always been difficult, and this remnant is part of the determined pioneer transportation system. There are several colorful points of interest to the south where the road climbs a long dugway to the sandy top of Haymaker Bench. "Thompson Turnover" is a steep section of chiseled steps where Thompson's wagon did not make the sharp bend and turned over. Another area with a grade in excess of thirty-five percent is known as "Peter's Whip-Up." The steep grade caused James C. Peters to whip his wagon team. The horses balked and he had to bring another team the following day to retrieve his wagon.

As you are dropping down, aim for the open wash to the south. That will give you a direct line to the creek. Dry Hollow is quite brushy along the banks, so cross immediately over to the north bank and climb above the vegetation. Traverse around the convoluted, narrow plunge that Dry Hollow makes at its mouth. It is an easy descent to Boulder Creek. Take

Lower Boulder Creek

another look at the waterfall from creek level; there is a grassy spot and pool at the mouth.

Heading downstream, the scenery is dominated by white, crossbedded rock domes. It is an easy scramble over the small saddle about one and a quarter miles down canyon. The way becomes quite brushy as the channel narrows. Progress is slow through this stretch as you work your way along the choked banks.

In the last mile before Boulder Creek is joined by Deer Creek, the character of the canyon changes drastically. Striated sandstone ledges appear along the banks and these gentle slopes make it an easy walk.

The canyon widens perceptibly at the junction of the two creeks. There is a small overhang on the west wall that makes for a good campspot. At two bends past the junction are the remains of an old gauging station. A dilapidated pair of hip waders and a shaky ladder complete the set. Sandstone ledges appear again but progress is slowed as you attempt to capture on film the black and red streaked patterns of the rock.

When the canyon heads due east, it is time for a decision. Around the corner the walls constrict and several deep plunge pools are formed by the trapped boulders. The last two of these will probably require swimming. There is an alternative route up and around these pools. Just before the south wall becomes totally straight, there is a steep slope that is possible to friction walk. There is a small vertical crack that marks the route. Directly opposite there is a long red bench just above stream level. If that bench starts pinching out and small sculptured alcoves appear at streamside, you've gone too far. At the top of the friction climb, a small dome will stick out to the east. To see the narrow section that is being avoided, go around the northern end of that dome and then head south. The views directly below are thrilling. Contouring in a westerly direction, there is a gradual slope back down to the creek. Cross over immediately to the east bank and there is a path for the next quarter mile.

Now the route alternates between easy benchland walking and route selection through the vegetation to affect a stream crossing. The winding course of the stream doubles back on itself several times. Then the canyon opens up with radiating side spurs to catch the eye.

The bright red berries on the lobed, current-type leaf belongs to a shrub called squawbush (Rhus trilobata). The berries are edible but quite tart. With the addition of sugar they can be made into a refreshing lemonade drink. In the fall the leaves turn red, and add their hue to the canyon country. The name comes from the fact that Indian women made extensive use of its stems in basketweaving. This plant is also known as skunkbush, descriptive of the scent given off by the crushed leaves.

In the bends of the last mile, the canyon walls have closed in again and the stream bubbles over small rock gardens. At each sharp bend, moss is growing against the canyon wall. There is a turn to the east and Boulder Creek joins the Escalante. The mouth is brushy.

If you decide to head upstream at this point, it is 5.7 miles of easy walking to reach Highway 12.

Mouth of Dry Hollow

TRAIL 10
UPPER CALF
CREEK FALLS

Difficulty: Strenuous
Length (one way):   2 miles
Time: ½ Day
Maps: Calf Creek 7.5
Water: Calf Creek

A short, steep scenic hike brings you to this waterfall, an excellent place to share a lunch and some time with a friend. Further exploration, both upstream and down, uncovers deep, inviting swimming holes.

Use the Highway 12 road log for exact mileages. Coming from Escalante, the road sits precariously on top of the Hogback. Just before the dirt road takes off to the left (milepost 81.6), the side drainage has cut back almost to the road. There was a BLM sign set back against the trees, but only a portion of the support posts remain.

From Highway 12, a short rocky road takes you through the pinyon pine (Pinus edulis) to a wide, sandy clearing. The trail takes off to the west next to the tallest pinyon tree at the edge of the dropoff. The state tree of New Mexico, the pinyon, burns with a pitchy, fragrant smell. Good crops of the edible nuts occur every three to four years.

To collect these nuts, you need several lawn chairs, a large tarp, several bags, a cooler full of beer, and some straws. Lay the tarp under the tree, set up the lawn chairs, and draw straws. The short straw climbs the tree and shakes the branches so that the pine nuts fall down while the rest of the group enjoys a cold one. This procedure is repeated at different trees until enough nuts have been collected.

The view from the edge is breathtakingly similar to those snatched along the Hogback and New Home Bench. Now there is time to focus on the mass of slickrock domes, mesas, and canyon walls. The whole hillside is covered with dark volcanic boulders. This tertiary addition occurred about 20 million years ago.

A discernable path has been created where the boulders have been moved to line the white sandstone slope. The BLM has cairned this route in the last two years in an attempt to curtail the multiple trails that lead across the sand. The path goes by a healthy stand of blue grama (Bouteloua gracilis) grass. These low clumps are easy to recognize in the fall because the seed head looks like a comb. The grama grasses are an important part of most western grazing ranges.

The trail goes right by a geological survey marker, then stays on the north side of the shallow draw. When trees are visible in the bowl further down this wash, the trail contours west along the hillside. When the streaked cliff face on the west wall of Calf Creek comes into focus, you should begin to hear the waterfall.

When the trail divides, the left sloping cairned route takes you around the point and down through the vegetation to the base of the falls. The higher trail continues to the head of the falls and several deep water pockets.

The shallow overhang on the eastern side is a good place to sit and view the falls. The path continues to the grassy bank at the edge of the pool. The walls around the falls contain hanging garden vegetation and many water streaks.

A short distance downstream, go around the pool and climb up to the cool, wet cave. Loren Eiseley said it best – "If there is magic on this earth, it lies in water." The falls and immediate surrounding area certainly contain a great deal of magic.

An excellent excursion is to follow Calf Creek for three miles downstream to the lip of Lower Calf Creek Falls. Most of the walk is in the stream, which has either a sandy or rippled sandstone bottom. Be aware of the carved out pockets that have been eroded in the bed. These can become a sudden wet encounter if you get too engrossed in the interplay of light and shadow.

The stream side has luxurious growths of watercress (Rorippa nasturtium-aquaticum). This member of the Mustard family is a welcome addition to wilderness salads. The common white flower that dots the bank is Siskiyou aster (Aster hesperius laetevirens).

The first two side streams add substantially to the flow of water. The rock outcropping at stream level has an asymmetrical arch. In a mile, a couple of blocks of sandstone have fallen into the stream. They don't completely block the channel so they are more a visual break than an impediment to travel.

At the first western break in the wall, a nice, sheltered sandbank occurs. The cool, shady area across the stream has created a suitable microhabitat for a Douglas-fir tree.

Just past the next western side draw, the streambed becomes boulder strewn and the banks get steeper. The increase in vegetation slows down progress, but a worn path on the eastern bank helps.

The final passageway before the waterfall is exciting. The stream cascades down a sandstone staircase as the walls constrict. Several deep pools have been carved out of the bedrock. A short swim is necessary to get through the last dark green pool. When that is accomplished, thirty feet more of walking brings you carefully to the edge of Lower Calf Creek Falls.

Water pocket filled with sticks

Deer Creek

TRAIL 11
DEER CREEK

Difficulty: Moderately Strenuous
Length (one way):   7.5 miles
Time: 8 Hours
Maps: King Bench 7.5
Water: Deer Creek

This challenging route requires some deep wading and negotiating brush thickets. The reward is an intimate association with a lively stream and a colorful canyon. Two continuation routes are possible. At the junction with Boulder Creek, you can head up Boulder Creek and return to the highway via Dry Hollow (Trail 9). If you continue down Boulder Creek (Trail 9), you can get to the highway by going up the Escalante River (Trail 7). Either of these continuations will comfortably make a two-day trip.

Follow the Burr Trail, the road which goes east to the Waterpocket Fold and the lower part of Capital Reef National Park, when it leaves Highway 12 at the southern end of Boulder. The first flowing stream the road crosses is Deer Creek, 6.5 miles from the turnoff. A BLM register is placed at the start of the primitive campground east of the creek. Park either at the campground or south of the road. The hiking route takes off south of the road along the streambank.

The area is quite green; the banks of the stream are covered with scouring rushes (Equisetum hyemale). These primitive aquatic plants can be separated from their close relatives, the sedges, by the following jingle: "Sedges have edges and rushes are round." Both of these plants have three ranked leaves. Because the scouring rushes contain high amounts of silica, the early settlers used them to clean their pots. Among the cattails (Typha latifolia) you may occasionally glimpse a red-winged blackbird (Agelaius phoeniceus). These melodic birds are easily identified by their bright red and yellow shoulder patch.

Either side of the stream can be the jumpoff point, but the west side offers a way along the sandy benches. This path can be followed for the first two miles, but when Deer Creek appears to run into Durffey Mesa, it is time to pick a route down to stream level. This can easily be done at the north side of the mouth of the second drainage coming in from the west.

The next mile or so of travel along the enclosed banks of the creek is heavily brushed and it is often simpler to walk in the center of the stream. Walking in the creek bed stirs up a lot of silt. This stream seems to have a great deal of sediment, but it will probably get scoured during the summer monsoons. This makes for a challenging passage as the bottom is not visible.

The creek makes several more attempts to cut into the mesa, but its convoluted path leads it in a southerly direction. There is only one pool that is over waist deep, but the cool, dark water and the enclosed walls did not reassure me that a swim was not in the forecast.

After several more sharp bends, there is a track on the west bank for a quarter mile. This easier route gives you an opportunity to take a better look at the striated walls. Another mile of walking brings you to a small arch formed in a slab of rock that appears to have fractured away from the west wall. On the opposite shelf, a toadstool rock has been carved out of the uneven-weathered sandstone.

The nature of the stream changes as it flows over fluted red ledges. The water feels warmer and is certainly shallower. Those little elongated black specks that are attached to the submerged rocks are the larval stage of aquatic insects.

The last side drainage coming in from the east before Boulder Creek is worth a brief side trip. Although there are adequate campsites at several spots along Deer Creek, the first really good spot is located against the west wall just past the junction with Boulder Creek. At this point, you have a choice of continuing down Boulder Creek to the Escalante River or heading up Boulder Creek. (See Trail 9.)

Lamanite Arch, Upper Gulch

Stream bed in Upper Gulch

TRAIL 12
UPPER GULCH

Difficulty: Moderate
Length (one way):   10 miles
Time: 1 Day
Maps: King Bench 7.5, Steep Creek Bench 7.5
Water: Water Canyon

This is one of the few hikes not aimed at getting to the Escalante River. The Wingate Cliffs give way to open sagebrush benches as this canyon cuts through the multi-colored Chinle Formation. A sharp contrast is provided by the narrow deep western side drainages. The last side canyon before Impossible Peak contains a massive arch.

Using the Burr Trail road log, the second stream crossing heading east from Boulder is The Gulch. The road descends sharply down to stream level, 10.7 miles east of the start of the Burr Trail.

Park by the trail register on the north side of the road. Walk up the road until it crosses the stream. Follow the tire tracks upstream. They'll veer left at Steep Creek, which enters on the left in less than a mile. Just before the mouth of this creek, there's a deep overhang on the west bank. It comes too early to be useful as a campsite, but the sight of a shelter is always a welcome sign when you're traveling light.

Side passages provide many of the scenic marvels on this hike. Steep Creek is a very long drainage and deserves a day or two of exploration. The next narrow opening entering from the west branches about a half mile up. There was a large tree trunk jammed below the left slot. (One of the many adventures to which I look forward is hiking the country above so that I can look down these pouroffs.)

The black streaks and orange patterns on the walls continue for another mile up the main canyon. You're forced to go around on the left when the water cuts through the Shinarump layer. The stairstep ends at a three foot waterfall. The sandy, steep arroyo is the exit route to get above this constriction. A fence across the wash is the first thing that greets you when you've climbed up. A much more open canyon awaits you. The Gulch goes through several bowknot meanders. Around the first bend there's a shallow cave cut out of the west wall, but cattle seem to have been the main visitors. The edge of the stream is a muddy bank.

When hiking this canyon, we saw the large three-inch tracks of a mountain lion (Felis concolor). This elusive nocturnal creature has been the basis of many myths. It is an effective predator, playing its part in "the balance of nature" by culling the weak and diseased deer. Although constantly hunted, this much maligned creature continues to share the wild,

91

Convolutions in Upper Gulch

open spaces. The Incas called this creature puma. Early settlers on the east coast called it panther, while it is known as cougar in the northwest.

There is a whole world of wonder right at your feet. The large four-toed and ridge-shaped heel pad of the mountain lion and the pinpoints and tail scrapes of the northern whiptail lizard (Cnemidophorus tigris septentrionalis) in the mud and sand expose a whole different world. Because most of the mammals are nocturnal, they are rarely seen. Even many of the other glimpses of wildlife are very fleeting. Deciphering these tracks can become an interesting game in unraveling the natural history of the creatures that inhabit these canyons. To a photographer, they also provide challenging form and texture photos.

Another short western branch appears in a quarter-mile. The main canyon continues to widen and serious benchland walking becomes the norm. These benches are covered with big sagebrush. This plant, the state flower of Nevada, thrives in deep, mildly basic soils. The small leaves, covered with grayish hairs, are adaptations for the retention of water under semiarid conditions. Belonging to the sunflower family, it does not follow the trends of most of the members by being insect pollinated but is instead wind pollinated. The genus name honors Artemisia, the wife of Mausolus, an ancient ruler in Asia Minor who had a magnificent monument erected in his memory. Artemesia is derived from Artemis, the Greek goddess of wild nature. The smell of the damp plant is a staple of the western mythos.

The next side branch, Water Canyon, provides the water flow for The Gulch. The streambed is filled with rushes and willows, which have been pushed down from a recent flashflood. About halfway up this deadend canyon, a huge cave hangs inaccessibly on the cliff face. The terminal alcove is covered with columbine, watercress, and cattails.

Egg Canyon appears in two and a half miles. The Wingate cliffs frame the upper reaches of the canyon, but the purple mounds and pedestal rocks dominate the foreground. Explore this dry eastern side drainage to uncover the reason for its name. A mile and a half up this wash, an old mining road becomes evident. At the crest of the hill, views of the Circle Cliffs and the Henry Mountains unfold.

Indian Trail Canyon appears on the left in another mile. A serious bushwack up this constricted streambed is necessary to get a view of Lamanite Arch. It is well worth the effort to make this trip. This inaccessible arch is certainly the highlight of the hike. There may be water flowing in this canyon. The high bench near the mouth is a good campsite.

Arroyo cutting is evident as you work your way up the meanders of The Gulch. Roads left from uranium exploration are numerous as you approach the boundary to Forest Service lands. The pack trail marked on the map is difficult to locate in its lower reaches. An exposed, eighteen foot pitch to get to the top of the Kayenta has a fixed rope dangling from the top. This is not the place to have an accident so I didn't try it. Climbing up to this spot, there's a triangular window in a separated slab of rock along the west wall of the immediate side gulch.

The jeep road continues up The Gulch, with views of Stair Canyon in the distance and the white dome of Impossible Peak to the west.

Halfway Hollow, The Gulch

TRAIL 13
THE GULCH

Difficulty: Moderately Strenuous
Length (one way):   12.5 miles
Time: 1½ Days
Maps: King Bench 7.5, Red Breaks 7.5
Water: The Gulch

This would be a moderate hike except for one exciting stretch. That stretch adds spice to this beautiful canyon walk. Extended trips (3 days) can be made by going up the Escalante River to Highway 12 or down the river and out Harrish Wash (4 days).

The directions to the trailhead are the same as for the previous hike. After parking by the trail register on the north side of the road, cross over to the sign on the south side.

From the trailhead sign, start down the west side of the flowing stream. There's a fence across the way in about an eighth of a mile. The route is quite obvious. Most of the time it looks like an old jeep road. The red layers of the Kayenta quickly dip underground, and the domes and striated patterns of the lighter Navajo sandstone dominate the view.

As you round the bend where the line camp is located on the west bank, there are a couple of caves carved out of the wall to the north. Just past the line camp on the west wall, similar pockets are found. One of these appeared to have a hawk's nest at the base. There are routes in and out of the canyon on both sides at this point. These are utilized by the stockmen to get cattle to their grazing areas.

Two more miles and the canyon bends sharply to the east. The west bank has a stand of medium-sized cottonwood trees. These trees can obscure the side drainage entering The Gulch. About an eighth of a mile up this long side draw a spring is located. The ground was wet and quicksand occurred in several places up this wash when I was there, but sand had covered any clear evidence of the spring.

If you continue around the bend past the location of the spring and past the fence, another half mile of walking will bring you to a deep natural tank. Although it did not look appetizing when I was there, this naturally carved out basin could be a refreshing swimming hole at the right time of year.

About a half-mile after The Gulch swings south again, a pedestal rock looms on the horizon. This marker signals a sharp bend in the passage.

Another mile of ambling brings another stock fence that stretches across the stream. This creates the upper portion of a holding area for cattle because a constriction and falls two miles downstream create a natural barrier. A trailer, line camp and corral are found just around the bend.

Narrows, Lower Gulch

The longest gopher snake (Pituophis melanoleucus) I have ever seen, over five feet long, was at this line camp. Even though I am a biologist, I decided not to handle that one; the sight of that large creature caused my heart to skip a beat.

The canyon narrows in another mile, and for the next half-mile you're caught between the sculptured walls as the stream cuts a way through. Right when there is a sharp turn to the east, the stream disappears down a constricted waterfall.

If you attempt these narrows, a piece of rope to lower your pack down will be of great benefit. The narrows continue for a quarter mile and the pool at the lower end may require a quick swim.

The first time I came to this notch where the water seems to disappear I tried to negotiate the sloping sandstone ledge so I could avoid the murky pool at the end of this constriction. When I fell twelve feet with my backpack into this narrow gorge, I broke my foot on a boulder at the bottom. I ended up having to swim the pool anyway. Three days later I managed to hobble the rest of the way down The Gulch, up the Escalante River to the highway and from there I managed to get the damage repaired.

The second time we laid logs across the first constriction and then carefully slid into the narrows about one-third of the way. It was a shallow wade the rest of the way.

The third time around, a route around the narrows was found. It is worthwhile to walk this far and evaluate the water flow, your ability, the time of year, take some pictures, and then decide whether to proceed or go back aways and around. The route around starts about a sixteenth of a mile back up the canyon where there is a shallow alcove on the west wall.

There is a break in the wall. I've placed a cairn topped with two black rocks on the first ledge about twenty feet above the streambed. There was a log jammed against the side of the wall but it's an easy friction climb to start up the sandstone. Continue up the layered sandstone until you're on Brigham Tea Bench. Catch your breath and enjoy the stupendous views in all directions. Head south until you can look due east into the narrows that you are skirting. Off to the right and below the rim are several green benches. The third one is your destination. At eye level, a distinct knoll will protrude to the southeast. Contour along the rim, walking on sand but staying away from the immediate edge.

There's a crack system that blocks further progress along the rim. This is the route down. Most of the way is simple. About two-thirds of the way down, which has been cairned, there's a small chimney where it is probably simpler to lower your pack down on a rope. This can be done in two stages if that's more comfortable. When you get to the level bench, locate the cairn at the east end that indicates the short step down to creek level. By all means, take the time to go back up through the narrows.

Halfway Hollow almost immediately enters from the north. This challenging passage does not go far until you hit a jump. Rumor has it that a route around the narrows to the east will lead into similar constricted pouroffs further up halfway Hollow.

When the canyon goes through a narrow portal, the jammed cottonwood log about fifteen feet up gives you a further reason to pause and reflect on the tremendous force of moving water. There are some possible campspots along this stretch and for the next half-mile past the northern side drainage. Then the canyon narrows again.

Another three miles bring you to a challenging side trip. Along this narrow side fissure you can find some vegetation not seen along the main stream.

The tall grass with the silky tuffs near the head is alkali sacaton (Sporobolus airoides). This grass has an open panicle, separating the seed grains along widely spreading branches.

Sacred datura (Datura metaloides) has long white funnel shaped flowers which open in the evening. The prickly berries are the fruits. All parts of this plant contain alkaloid poisons but the psychedelic qualities were used by Indians in their religious ceremonies.

Before you have gone a half-mile up this crack, climb out the south side and across the short sandstone ridge to the next fissure. Follow this one back down to The Gulch.

There are plenty of campsites in the next mile of easy walking down to the Escalante River. The junction of the two streams is crowded with willows.

Escalante River at Horse Canyon

Holes in the wall, Horse Canyon

TRAIL 14
HORSE CANYON

Difficulty: Moderately Easy
Length (one way):   13 miles
Time: 1½ Days
Maps: Wagon Box Mesa 15, King Bench 7.5, Red Breaks 7.5
Water: Springs, Lower Horse Canyon, Escalante River

This is the first of the canyons that drains the Circle Cliff Upwarp. The Circle Cliffs were uplifted during the Laramide Orogeny, which lasted from 50 to 80 million years ago. The present Rocky Mountains were formed during this time, and, closer to our area, the San Rafael Swell was uplifted. Wide near the head where it cuts through the easily erodable Chinle Formation; by the time Horse Canyon joins the Escalante it is enclosed by impressive walls. This long hike offers several exit routes pioneered by the cattlemen which bring you to the higher benchlands.

Head east from Boulder on the Burr Trail for 19.3 miles. The road drops into the Circle Cliffs basin. Turn right on the dirt road by the BLM sign indicating the way to the Wolverine Petrified Wood area. Continue for

5.7 miles on this road until the wash turns west and the road starts to climb up the hill. The side road heading west down Horse Canyon may be too sandy so a higher parking spot can be found by crossing the wash and pulling off the side of the road as it turns sharply east. The start of the route is down the broad cottonwood lined wash. All that is left of the line camp on the right are the wheels of an old caboose.

It looks like Horse Canyon is going to go straight through the Circle Cliffs to the west but the draw veers sharply to the south. It remains a wide wash until you pass the old mining claim marker, a white rectangle painted on the rock. The uranium boom in the 1950s brought extensive exploration throughout the area. The Bonneville Company did extensive drilling in Horse Canyon. Mine activity lasted from 1952-56.

Chunks of petrified wood can be found in the streambed. At the first side draw coming in from the east, there is a nice oak grove at the mouth. This side slot is boulder strewn at the lower end, making it a challenge to explore. The air is filled with common flickers (Colaptes auratus).

As the canyon starts to meander, the displays of desert varnish highlight the walls. Two miles of these twists and there are a couple of windows sculpted out of the sandstone cliff. A stock fence is strung across the wash around the next bend.

This signals the start of a narrow section. The next side slot plunges dramatically into Horse Canyon through a cleft in the cliff about thirty feet above the canyon floor. Going around the next rock outcropping, you pass by a display of little arches, alcoves, and other scooped-out pockets along the west wall.

This brief and intense passage ends quickly and the wash opens up again. There's a path that can be followed that the cattle have trampled down. This cuts off the meanders of the wash. A line camp with a photogenic stove sits at the base of a route out the east wall. Take care not to disrupt anything. Not only are these line camps a part of the pioneer history of the area, but many of them are still used today.

Wolverine Creek (Trail 15) comes in after three more bends. This canyon can be used as an easy exit route if you want to make a short loop.

The wide sandy spaces last for another half-mile and then sagebrush covers the sand benches. Around a sharp bend, there's an overhang on the northwest wall that makes an excellent camp spot. The shallow overhang has several Fremont barberry bushes (Berberis fremontii) that act as vegetative screening. The fragrance from the small, yellow flowers is an added treat. Also known as holly-grape, this is the state flower for Oregon. The small, dark blue berries can be made into excellent jams and jellies. A yellow dye is made from the roots and stems.

Across the way is a pack trail climbing up the hillside. When the trail forks, either direction takes you to a spring. there is a line camp by the right route. The spring on the left is developed and generally has a better flow. Continue on the pack trail past the water trough until it breaks to the top of Little Bown Bench for a larger view.

In the next bend of Horse, surface water appears. Another line camp is found to the right. Bales of hay are wedged into a shallow overhang.

Line camp, Horse Canyon

At the fence just around the next bend, a BLM road closure sign ends four-wheel-drive travel down the canyon. Another half-mile and the mouth of Little Death Hollow (Trail 16) appears from the east. The generator and sections of old pipe were part of an attempt to get water for cattle up to Big Bown Bench. Another fence spans Horse Canyon a quarter-mile further down.

The next short fissure entering from the east is choked with vegetation. The upper portion is boulder strewn.

From here, another fifteen minutes of walking brings you to the wide junction with the Escalante River.

TRAIL 15
WOLVERINE CREEK

Difficulty: Moderate
Length (one way):   5 miles
Time: ½ Day
Maps: Wagon Box Mesa 15, King Bench 7.5
Water: Bring your own; intermittent in Middle Wolverine
Canyon

This area is noted for its black petrified wood and a portion was set aside by the BLM as an outstanding natural area. The lower portion has extensive honeycombed walls. A challenging loop trip can be made by going down Little Death Hollow (Trail 16) and returning up the south arm of Wolverine.

Use the Burr Trail road log for mileages. Go east on the Burr Trail until the BLM sign for Wolverine appears. Turn south on this road. Right after the road goes through the narrow wash of upper Wolverine canyon, the country opens and there is a large sign identifying the Wolverine Petrified Wood Natural Area. The route starts at the BLM sign detailing the scenic qualities of the area and reminding visitors that this area is closed to

Petrified wood, Wolverine Canyon

Wolverine Canyon

collecting. The black petrified wood attracts the eye because the purple and lavender hills provide such a vibrant backdrop. Climb over the fence where the steps are provided.

The first mile and a half of easy walking take you through the Circle Cliffs and a junction with the most northerly arm. Petrified wood pieces are scattered throughout the hillsides. It is easiest to cut across the benches rather than follow the meanders of the wash.

Turning south, another mile and the south fork joins Wolverine Creek. The gray beds at the junction provide a good seat for a pause in which to gaze at the cliffs starting to surround you.

Intermittent water occurs shortly down canyon, creating conditions for cottonwoods and other riparian plants to appear. Two large alcoves have been eroded out of the northern bends.

The walls of the lower canyon are highly eroded with small pockets. Some of these are deep enough to sit in. These windows and honeycombed basins look like scoops have been taken out of the sandstone walls. Vertical cracks take the eye to the sky and stain patterns higher up.

The last half mile doubles back on itself and the sand slows down the pace. The canyon opens just as it joins Horse Canyon.

All photos Little Death Hollow

TRAIL 16
LITTLE DEATH
HOLLOW

Difficulty: Strenuous
Length (one way):   7.5 miles
Time: ½ Day
Maps: Wagon Box Mesa 15, Moody Creek 15, Red Breaks 7.5
Water: Bring your own

Although this canyon is named Death Hollow, its name has been altered to differentiate it from the much longer and more strenuous canyon (Trail 2) draining the Aquarius Plateau. This hike does offer a superb section of narrows, an oval arch, an extremely tight lateral passage, and Indian petroglyphs.

Follow the road log for the previous hike. Continue past the petrified wood area for 2.8 miles. The road crosses the upper part of Little Death Hollow. Take the short spur west to the corral. The route starts by the corral just off of the road. After crossing the fence, stay on the grassy area to the right (north) of the wash. Juniper and sage dot the landscape. In a mile and a half of easy walking the south fork joins the arroyo. Another mile and a narrower, convoluted channel dominates, with colorful sandstone walls enclosing the canyon.

There are lateral joints leading away from the main canyon. Look for the oval arch in one of the remnant fins left between two of these parallel fissures. It's one of those sights that holds you because it is a superlative in an already highly scenic area.

After a few more twisting meanders, a narrow slot appears on the north wall. You can climb over the first blockage and continue around the bend. The next slot is sloped as it winds around the curve, calling for a sideways stemming technique.

The walls of the main canyon stay straight, but the wash bottom narrows to a six foot width. We were surprised to see a kangaroo rat (Dipodomys ordi) hopping down the narrow channel. This rodent has evolved so that it is able to survive in a desert environment. It has no need for drinking water, since it manufactures its own water from the seeds that it eats. Spacious, convoluted chambers behind the nose condense water vapor from the air. It's erratic hopping makes it difficult to capture and fun to watch.

For the next mile and a half, the canyon remains one serious constriction. Earlier flows of water have created log james above your head, some of them twenty-five feet above the canyon floor. Several of these

Arch in Little Death Hollow

lower piles would have been more challenging if the scooped out area below them had been filled with water. Lateral fracture lines provide access points to higher ground, but the ledges are not continuous down canyon so they do not create an alternate route.

Up to this point, the streambed itself has been fairly flat and gravely. Now the passage becomes blocked by large boulders. One of these purple chockstones was easier to negotiate by going under it.

The final two boulder jams were created by grayish, limestone slabs. When you come to the one that requires a ten-foot down-climb, a somewhat tricky scramble up the north wall to a wide ledge is the route. If you continue past this barrier, the next chockstone has a dark pool of undetermined depth twelve feet directly below it. The ledge provides an easy bypass around this pool until it slopes back down to the canyon floor.

The drainage widens and in another mile you pass under an old pipeline that carried water up to Big Bown Bench. The wide mouth of Little Death Hollow bears little resemblance to the just completed narrows. The junction with Horse Canyon is the first safe place to camp.

Silver Falls Canyon

TRAIL 17
SILVER FALLS
CREEK

Difficulty: Moderate
Length (one way): 8.5 miles
Time: 1 Day
Maps: Moody Creek 15
Water: Lower Silver Falls Creek and the Escalante River

This beautiful canyon was part of the Hall's Crossing road that was used to get to southeastern Utah after the Hole-in-the-Rock route was abandoned. The transformation from wide wash to narrow canyon is typical for the canyons draining the Circle Cliffs. The lower portion of the canyon is adorned with great streaks of desert varnish, giving this canyon its name.

There are two roads off the Burr Trail that lead to the Silver Falls turnoff. The first road turns south at the Wolverine Petrified Wood sign

G. B. Hobbs inscription, Silver Falls Canyon

and passes the trailheads of the previous three hikes. The second road leaves the Burr Trail 10.9 miles past the Wolverine sign and heads south. There is a sign indicating that this road goes to Moody Canyon. The two roads join together shortly before the turnoff to Silver Falls. Continue south for 2.7 miles after the two roads come together.

When the road follows the streambed, assess any damage done by recent flooding. In another mile, the corral on the right is a good place to park. Four-wheel-drive vehicles could get to the NPS sign, but you would miss the first area of windows.

This whole canyon used to be a four-wheel-drive route that connected with Harris Wash as a cross canyon trail. With the passage of legislation authorizing Glen Canyon National Recreation Area, this road is now closed. When you add the effects of the normal erosional processes, this is now a fascinating hike.

Just past the corral, the old jeep road climbs up the hill to avoid a meander of the drainage that plunges through and over the gray Shinarump bedrock. This half-mile bend is an eroded wonderland of windows and scooped out pockets in the rocks. Explore this without a backpack as it takes a scramble to get down the first dropoff.

Following the road, the purple, red, grey, and green shades of the exposed oxides of the iron-bearing minerals create a lively background. This rock layer also contains uranium ore, so there was intense exploration and mining activity in the 1950s wherever this formation was exposed at the surface. The rock cairns are old mining claim boundary markers.

Shortly after the north fork comes in the GCNRA sign is visible. The rising walls of Wingate come closer together. It seems like an anomaly that this is the same rock formation that is perched high above stream level just a few miles back. The area of the Circle Cliffs is an upwarp, which means that the land has been raised.

Just as the walls and the silence start to close in, a half-dozen cackling ravens (Corvus corax) pass by overhead. These opportunistic scavengers are very common. Continuing deeper into the canyon, you pass by a rincon on either side. These high and dry meanders are part of the readable history of the stream. The spring marked on the topographic map is just a slight seep but water does appear shortly down canyon.

In another mile the Hobbs inscription and memorial plaque are found in an overhang on the west wall. George Brigham Hobbs was with the Hole-in-the-Rock expedition and was one of the four scouts sent to explore the unknown country east of the Colorado River. He was taking supplies to the settlers at Bluff in February of 1883 when he was caught in a snow storm. Figuring that his time had come, he pecked his name in the sandstone. He survived and was able to complete his journey.

In the last two miles the canyon widens, and benches that are suitable campsites appear. The line camp on the right means the river is a quarter of a mile away.

Formation in Silver Falls Canyon

109

TRAIL 18
MOODY CANYON

Difficulty: Moderately Strenuous
Length (one way):   7 miles
Time: 1 Day
Maps: Moody Creek 15, Hall Mesa 15
Water: Escalante River

This canyon provides access into the lower part of the Escalante River. The colorful hills near the mouth give way to a boulder strewn canyon. A long side trip up Middle Moody Canyon is a combination of narrows and expansive views of the purple hills, Deer Point, and other eroded features.

Road directions are the same as the previous hike. At the junction to Silver Falls Creek, continue straight (left) for another 9.3 miles to the corral and line camp. The Burr Trail road log has a more detailed description.

When the road enters the creek bed a high profile vehicle may be necessary. If the gravel bottom looks smooth, continue for another two miles until you see the line camp and corral. Park on the road leaving the creekbed on the left. There may be some water flowing but it quickly dries up.

The wash is quite wide as you start hiking west. The multi-colored hills are topped with white monoliths. The wash will stay open until after the junction with Middle Moody. After two and a half miles of walking, a box canyon comes in from the west. Seasonal water pockets may be found about half way up this short draw. Another mile and there is an arch just past the mouth of the next side arm. One more mile and the wide entrance to Middle Moody Canyon appears.

If you are not intent on reaching the Escalante River, this side canyon offers plenty of challenging hiking and lots of color. The spring shown on the map is barely a wet spot but there may be water about a quarter mile further up in the first eastern indentation.

(This side canyon remains a wide wash for the first three and a half miles but there is a boulder strewn section just before the next side draw. The wash curves around the large colorful dome. The harder Shinarump Conglomerate member of the Chinle Formtion acts as a caprock. Pedestal formations line the wash. As the wash widens again, the sandy shelves are covered with cheatgrass (Bromus tectorum), tumbleweed (Salsola kali), and rabbit brush. Cheatgrass was brought over from Europe and has now spread over much of the United States. The clay hills to the north are a kaliedoscope of colors.

Just before the narrows, there is a remnant of an old mining road on the north side of the wash. The canyon takes an abrupt turn to the north at

Middle Moody Canyon

the point. If this first section is muddy, there is a shelf which skirts this constricted fifteen-foot-wide passage. This light gray rock is the more resistant Shinarump Conglomerate.

As the walls rise higher, the wash opens up a bit. Utah juniper and Apache-plume (Fallugia paradoxa) cover the slopes. Exercise care in this area as there are lots of rocks on the floor of the wash. It is always the one that looks the most stable that moves when you step on it. One short stretch had quantities of young tamarisks sprouting along the wash. this exotic has spread to the furthest reaches of the side drainages of the Colorado River since it was first brought over from the Mediterranean region.

At the fork (not the short side arm where the canyon heads north again) the left branch is the main one. There is a brief burst of red and purple shales at stream level, but stream debris quickly cover most of the color. Fallen boulders also add to the challenge of finding a route. Then the streambed composition changes to brown ledges with fossilized ripple marks. Hard to imagine this area under water.

Tracks of bighorn sheep (Ovis canadensis) were found in the soft mud. These sheep have been transplanted into the Escalante area from the upper portions of Lake Powell. Radio telemetry was used to monitor their condition. The State of Utah Division of Wildlife Resources has also utilized recent aerial counts and has found that the sheep are expanding their range.

After two more miles of travel the walls diminish in height. I scrambled

111

Deer skull

up the wall right to the flat area above. If you stay in the wash, two more miles will bring you to the base of Deer Point.

On top, a whole different landscape of white unfolds. There are many shallow erosional patterns on this relatively flat area between the east arm and the main drainage. In the fall, these shallow draws are filled with the yellows and reds of gamble oak and squawbush. Following one of these, it ended abruptly at the lip of the main arm.)

Back in the Moody Creek drainage, the Wingate sandstone encloses the canyon for the remaining three miles. There are several stretches where big blocks have fallen from the walls but a way through them is easily found. After the last boulder field, the channel straightens and you can hear the river. Camping is best near the mouth or at the junction with Middle Moody Canyon.

This series of canyons that drain the southern part of the Circle Cliffs were named after an Escalante stockman, John Moody.

TRAIL 19
HARRIS WASH

Difficulty: Moderately easy
Length (one way): 10.3 miles
Time: 1 to 2 Days
Maps: Red Breaks 7.5, Moody Creek 15
Water: Harris Wash

This is a premier hike, recommended for young adults. A colorful canyon, Harris Wash provides easy access to the Escalante River. In the 1880s, this wash was part of a wagon route that led to a ferry at the mouth of Hall's Creek. There are plenty of good campsites along its winding path. This canyon is a favorite entrance route for longer trips down the Escalante River.

Go down the Hole-in-the-Rock road for 10.8 miles. The Hole-in-the-Rock road is 5.1 miles east of Escalante and 23.2 miles west of Boulder. There is a BLM sign marking the left hand turn to the trailhead. Staying left, 6.3 miles puts you at the trail register at Harris Wash.

From the trail register, head down the jeep road that follows the main wash. In a half-mile there is a fence across the wash. The gate is on the north end of the fence. The surrounding country is wide open, with the red carmel formation much in evidence. Another mile and the National Park Boundary Fence appears. The gate is on the south side of the wash.

Water starts flowing in the streambed at this point. In the spring the banks are lined with smooth scouring rushes (Equisetum laevigatum) and field horsetails (Equisetum arvense). These waterloving plants provide a green tone to the streambed.

The rapid transformation of open wash to canyon occurs because the stream is downcutting through a more resistant rock layer. In another two miles a large stone fin projects from the north wall and constricts the passage to ten feet. The immediate draw to the south invites exploration. We spotted a gopher snake just before the fluted dry waterfall. A nonpoisonous snake, it is sometimes mistaken for a rattlesnake because of its diamond-shaped markings and behavioral traits of hissing and vibrating its tail.

As the canyon walls get higher, the winding path of the stream has cut deep overhangs. Water seeps are common along the walls of these alcoves. The sandy benches left by these meanders make excellent campsites. The attractive streaks running down the walls are called desert varnish. The Indians labeled this same phenomenon patina or nature painting. The brown to black oxide stains of iron or manganese took centuries to produce. While water obviously plays a part in the creation of these streaks, the exact process is not completely understood.

Harris Wash

Pool at end of side canyon, Harris Wash

Moqui steps, Harris Wash

114

Pool in side canyon, Harris Wash

Time goes by steadily as the walking pace is slowed to allow the senses to absorb the patterns created in this winding canyon. After three more miles a flow of water enters on the south side. This side draw is easy to miss if you are taking the high and dry path on the north side, but if you're following the stream the mouth is readily visible. The bench with oak trees is a good campsite. A deep swimming hole at the first bend up this draw is an added attraction.

The next southern side-draw awaits exploration by those willing to work through the vegetation.

Another two twisting miles and a large isolated butte of sandstone on the skyline ahead indicates the junction of Harris Wash and the Escalante River.

Harris Wash was named after an early cattle man named Jimmy L. Harris. A.H. Thompson, searching for an overland route to the Dirty Devil river in 1872, called it False Creek. When the Hole-in-the-Rock route was abandoned due to lack of business, Charles Hall pioneered a wagon road to a new and easier ferry site. He operated the ferry at the mouth of Hall's Creek from 1881-84. The wagon route went down Harris Wash, up Silver Falls Creek, through the Circle Cliffs, down Muley Twist Canyon through the Water Pocket Fold, and then down Hall's Creek to its mouth at the Colorado River.

Pool and stains, Red Breaks

TRAIL 20
RED BREAKS

Difficulty: Strenuous
Length (one way): 13 miles
Time: 1 to 2 Days
Maps: Red Breaks 7.5
Water: Bring your own and seasonal water pockets

Off the beaten path, this area offers the challenge of narrow slot canyons, expanded vistas, and exciting cross-terrain travel. It is an area of varied and bright colors, as indicated by the name. Truly a place for those who want room to roam.

Follow the Hole-in-the-Rock road log. Directions are the same as the previous hike. The route starts at the Harris Wash trailhead sign. Instead of continuing down the wash, follow the jeep road heading north. After it crosses the Harris drainage, the road will climb out of the wide sandy wash coming down from the north. The jeep road continues out to an area called the "V." That area was named the "V" from the angle that Harris makes when it joins the Escalante River.

When you continue up the wash, the red colored land is rising away from you toward the west. The walls quickly close in, and a jump blocks further wash travel in about a half-mile. A short scramble up the steep, eastern stairstep-wall gets you around the barrier. Bring a short piece of rope with you as it will be easier to lower your pack down before making the descent.

Almost immediately there is a junction. Take the right fork up this area of smooth layered rocks. For the next mile the wash alternates between a sand and willow-lined bottom and sculptured rock. Finally the walls constrict so close together it's time to climb up on the right until you hit a shelf.

Carefully walk on this ledge. The views below of the slot canyon indicate an extremely tight and possible wet walk for those intent on exploring this channel. Definitely try it without the encumbrance of a pack. In a half-mile you can look across the narrow gorge to the abrupt end of a side drainage.

At the next fork a decision needs to be made concerning the route of further travel. Three choices will be outlined. There is a bit of an overhang large enough for a small party that can be used as a base camp if more than one day is going to be spent exploring the area. The first route stays on the benchland on the east side of the branch heading northeast. The walls open up in a quarter-mile and there is a slickrock descent to the level wash. Now the walking becomes somewhat easier, alternating between a wide sandy wash and slickrock. There are some interesting windblown patterns to catch and hold the eye. For the next two and a half miles, the skyline is a series of buttes, turrets and domes; a hobbitland display of Navajo sandstone.

At the head of the wash, where it disappears into the rocky slopes, angle north (left) and up to the dome almost directly in front of you. Skirting it on the west side, there's a shallow pass that allows access to a viewpoint. Below the sloping sandstone ledges are several large, bare sand dunes. Across this open area is a domed area of joints that radiate away from the Escalante River. The laccolithic Henry Mountains rise starkly, far to the north.

The second way can be used as part of a loop continuation of the first route. At the east branch junction, drop down just above its mouth. Although it is possible to slide down into the left branch at this point, it is safer and easier to immediately climb up the point between the two forks. Staying to the west, about 80 feet above the wash, there's an easy slickrock descent in a quarter-mile. You've passed the first side arm coming in from the west.

Once you're at the bottom, the amount of time since the last rain will determine how easy and dry your walk up the draw will be. In a mile of walking, there is another spur coming in from the west. A short distance up this is a small natural bridge.

The first pouroff up the main arm can be bypassed on the west side. The next constriction can be circumvented on either side. The upper portion is so narrow that you can easily step over the slot.

One more western side drainage comes in, and then a series of waterpockets require slickrock walking. At the head of this wash, a walk up the tiered sandstone will bring you to the same place as the first route. You need to veer slightly to the east and around the right side of the lower knob.

The third route also goes up this western arm. After the initial descent down into the wash, immediately ascend the western side of the drainage. Contour along the western side of the rim, climbing up to the mesa top. Continuing in a northwesterly direction will put you along the rim of the arm with the natural bridge at its mouth. Follow the rim until there is a safe place to cross.

Due west of you a red knoll (X6316) breaks the skyline. This point is a mile away and about a five hundred foot gain in elevation. Route selection through the broken red country is up to the individual. A panoramic view presents itself as you stand on the edge of this sandstone escarpment.

Careful orienteering is necessary to find your way back. The drainages and benches look very similar. Make sure you stay far enough north to pass the head of that first side draw.

Narrows, Red Breaks

TRAIL 21
ESCALANTE RIVER—
HARRIS WASH TO
LAKE POWELL

Difficulty: Moderately Strenuous
Length (one way):   42.8 miles
Time: 8 Days
Maps: Moody Creek 15, King Mesa 7.5, The Rincon 15
Water: Escalante River, various side drainages

This long hike can last even longer if the many tributaries are also explored. The river canyon changes from wide benches to almost barren banks to an extremely challenging boulder-strewn section. This hike takes long enough to allow the canyon pace to envelop you. If the lake level rises above 3700 feet, the mouth of Coyote Wash will be flooded and the highline trail (Trail 29) just past the mouth of Stevens becomes the exit route.

Entrance to this hike comes from the Escalante River below Calf Creek (TRAIL 7), Silver Falls Creek (TRAIL 17), or Harris Wash (TRAIL 19).

Wall detail, Harris Wash

Downstream from Harris Wash the river continues to meander, leaving broad sandy areas on which to walk. The river is cutting through the softer Kayenta Formation, which is topped by domes of Navajo sandstone. The purple of the Kayenta is offset by the light green stems of Mormon tea (Ephedra viridis). These plants are first cousins to the pines and junipers. The common name is derived from brewing the tops into a drink used as a cough medicine. The drug ephedrine, used in the treatment of hay fever and colds, is obtained from some of the Asian species.

Your gentle progress along one of these benches may be interrupted by the sudden bounding gait of a blacktail jackrabbit (Lepus californicus). This hopper can move at speeds up to 35 mph. The distinctive tracks show the hind feet first, followed by the unevenly spaced front paws. These hares occupy forms, or shallow depressions, rather than burrows. Their long ears are used as a thermoregulator, dissipating heat in the hot summer months.

The first western tributary appears in five and a half miles. Fence Canyon is easily recognizable by the line camp sitting high on the bluff. There is water flowing from this canyon and there are campsites at the mouth and in shallow overhangs just past the mouth. The river no longer flows the same channel as shown on the topographic map, and now crowds the western bank at the mouth of Fence. A short tight passage on the west wall brings you to the next level sandy bench.

The Wingate sandstone frames the lower canyon walls. This colorful reddish, rust to brown sandstone will become impossing cliffs as the river continues downcutting. There is a well-worn path to follow, but the brushy streambanks impede crossing from one side to the other.

Another noxious weed that scratches the legs is rattleweed milkvetch (Astragalus praelongus). A tall branching plant with cream colored flowers, the dry seed pods rattle when you pass by. Clumps of spike dropseed (Sporobolus contractus) dot the sandy areas. This one-to-two foot tall grass ends in a sheathed, contracted, dense pannicle of seeds. In Mesa dropseed (Sporobolus flexuosus) the seedhead is spread in an open pannicle.

In sharp contrast to the open feeling along the river, the side arms are narrow. These side branches provide a variety of experiences. Some go for a long distance, others end abruptly. Boulder strewn, dry washes, or sculpted slickrock, each has its own appeal. There is an excellent campspot among the oaks near the mouth of the last eastern (northern) slot before Twentyfive mile wash.

The mouth of Twentyfive mile appears around the next bend as another water source. This canyon (Trail 23) is a moderately easy exit route to the Hole-in-the-Rock road.

The first recorded traverse of the whole canyon occurred in 1939. Three Brigham Young University students were guided by Jess Barker of Escalante. They walked from Calf Creek to the Colorado River and then along the bank of the river to Hole-in-the-Rock Crossing. Here they installed a bronze plaque commemorating the trek of the San Juan Mission. The plaque was moved to the top of the notch when Lake Powell was formed.

Another six miles of meanders brings you to Moody Canyon (Trail 18). The term "meander" is derived from the Meander River of Asia Minor, whose lower reaches have an extremely twisty course. Two more bends and a deeply cut overhang marks the mouth of East Moody Canyon. There are plenty of places to camp in the sand. Water should appear in the bed of this tributary before you've gone a half-mile. Several days can be spent exploring, but the conchoidal fracture displays in the Wingate walls appear a short distance up this canyon. The carved lines look like a shell, hence the name.

A half-mile downstream the river has cut through the neck of a meander, leaving a rincon. The river is quite convoluted through this section.

Scorpion Gulch (Trail 26) is a narrow opening to the west. Good campsites are found on the sand bar at the mouth. This is another clear water source. Cattails abound in the lower end of Scorpion.

The next eastern draw is known locally as Georgie's Camp, named after Escalante stockman Georgie Davis. Sand dunes dominate the scenery as the canyon widens and the Wingate cliffs recede. One of the few grasses able to grow on these sandy slopes is Indian ricegrass (Oryzopsis hymenoides). This grass is an extremely valuable forage plant in the semiarid west. Also used as a food source by the Indians, it was usually ground into flour and made into bread. Purple and maroon shales appear at streamside. The scenery becomes starker, and vegetation is much reduced.

For several miles this colorful display holds sway. Then around a bend a high ridge parallels the northern bank. The cliffs can be seen a half-mile behind this ridge. This pile of rock reminded me of a lateral morrain left by glacial action. That certainly did not cause the deposition of this feature.

The next northern wash did not get explored very far due to the heat, but looked enticing for a future trip. After the next bowknot bend, only a low ridge and a caprock mark the meander.

Travel down the Escalante River for fun and adventure started earlier than most people realize. In 1948, Harry Aleson and Georgie White Clark took the first rubber raft trip down the Escalante. The pair had numerous adventures dealing with the changing volume of stream flow. It took them seven days to drag and float down to the swollen Colorado River, and only two more days to go to Lee's Ferry.

Not only for the boaters, but for hikers, the river channel becomes a test of navigational skills. Known as "The Narrows," the next five miles are extremely challenging. The way is blockaded by large boulders that have broken off the walls. A whole day can be consumed finding a way up, around, or through this boulder stretch. It is more difficult to read the river as it threads its way through these obstructions. At one crossing, I went in one step from knee-deep to chest-deep water.

The side drainages are also boulder scrambles. Just above Stevens, the canyon assumes a less broken appearance, and willow covered banks line the stream.

Stevens Canyon is the narrow defile entering from the east. It is named for Al Stevens, who grazed cattle southwest of the Henry Mountains. A

Stevens Arch, Escalante River

short side hike up this canyon and a pool fills the constricted channel. A scramble up the wall brings you to a ledge that bypasses the pool. As the ledge drops away, work through the willows to the cottonwood log jammed against the other wall. This precarious climb allows you to circumvent the next pool. Several more bends brings you to a dramatically carved natural bridge. The mossy wall next to it is known as "The Grotto." A small break in the moss has enough room to catch the dropping water.

Most people head up Coyote Gulch (Trail 29), which appears in two more bends. (If the lake level has flooded the mouth of Coyote Gulch, the high line trail (Trail 29) climbs up the first draw past Stevens and drops down farther up into Coyote Gulch.) If you want to see what happens when a river runs into a lake, continue down canyon. The most noticeable change is that it becomes exceedingly difficult to judge the safest place to walk. Quicksand is everywhere as the stream drops its sediment load. Dead trees are another indication of the fluctuating lake level. Serious log jams can occur, impeding boat passage from Lake Powell.

A very strenuous route out can be taken up the "Crack-in-the-Wall" trail (Trail 30). This huge sandslide can be a serious trudge with gear.

Devils Garden formations

TRAIL 22
DEVIL'S GARDEN

Difficulty: Moderately easy, recommended for children
Length (one way):   ¼ mile
Time: 1 Hour to ½ day
Maps: Seep Flat 7.5
Water: Bring your own

This is a fairyland area of small knobs, arches, and other eroded landforms. The BLM recognized the scenic special features of the area and designated it as an outstanding natural area. A great place to lose yourself in flights of fantasy.

Go down the Hole-in-the-Rock road for 12.7 miles. A BLM sign signals the short road to the right. The parking area for Devil's Garden occurs in .3 miles.

From the parking lot, strike out in a southerly direction. There is no trail, you can let the scenery and the topography be your guide. Mano arch is one of the many geological features to be viewed. It is found a short distance south of the parking lot. These structures were formed due to a difference in the erosional rate of the different rock layers. A more resistant cap layer has protected the underlying softer rock, thus creating the many varied pinnacles.

This is an excellent area for a picnic and as much leisurely exploring as the family or group desire. A stroll around this area is unique among the outlined hikes of this guide book because there is no set distance to go or any predetermined objective.

126

TRAIL 23
TWENTYFIVE MILE
WASH

Difficulty: Moderate
Length (one way):   13.1 miles
Time: 1 to 2 Days
Maps: Sunset Flat 7.5, Moody Creek 15
Water: Lower Twentyfive Mile Wash

Walking down this route allows you to witness the transformation of a wash into a canyon. Through the length of this canyon four rock layers are exposed. Starting with the red Carmel formation, all three members of the Glen Canyon Group (Navajo, Kayenta, and Wingate) are visible. The side canyons give this hike numerous scenic digressions.

Use the Hole-in-the-Rock road log. Turn left at the "Egypt" sign. When the road crosses Twentyfive Mile Wash in 3.7 miles, there is a BLM sign on the north side of the road to mark the parking area. The route heads directly down the bottom of the wash. If the wash has recently flooded, it might be advisable to park on the flats before the road drops down to cross the wash. (That is what happened the last time I did this hike.)

The focus for the first couple of miles was observing and photographing the interchange of colors left by the flood. Most of the wash was gray, with pink to reddish mudbanks left at the higher spots. The distinct cracking patterns left by the drying mud also captures the eye.

Since this early open section of wash is usually dry, the walking is easy. Sparse streamside vegetation in the fall consists of golden rabbitbrush and Apache-plume. The rabbitbrush has a dense cluster of tubular yellow flowers that blanket this shrub in the fall. Rabbits eat the foliage and seeds, hence the name. The Hopi used the stripped branches for basket making. Apache-plume, a member of the rose family, also attains its showiest stage in the fall. Another common name, feather duster bush, comes from the cluster of featherly-tailed fruits that linger on the bush.

After three miles of hiking, a narrow side crack comes in from the north. Someone had built a cairn on the shelf by the mouth. It boxes out fairly quickly in a dramatic dry waterfall. The upper portion of this narrow, deep defile is accessible from the Egypt road. We walked the rim and then traveled cross-country until we found a route down into the next side drainage. This type of day travel is only for skilled and confirmed desert rats.

There's another short northern side arm just before a sizable dome that dominates the right side of the wash. This one also ends in a jump. The

Narrows and pool, side canyon of Twentyfive Mile Wash

differential erosional qualities of the same rock layer are a constant source of amazement and joy.

One more mile brings you to another side drainage. Wide at its mouth, the main or left branch is walkable for at least a mile. It does require climbing around a couple of scooped-out pools. The right arm pinches into a tortuous wet passage around the first bend.

The sandy bends of the main streambed have been covered with tansy-aster (Machaeranthera linearis). Although related to true asters, these plants are widely branched. Yellow centered, the brilliant purple ray flowers are what catch the eye.

Although this wash has dropped quickly enough to give the semblance of a canyon, the walls are only about 60 feet high. Sometimes there is water flowing in the streambed past this side canyon, but generally you can expect to travel for another five miles or so before the stream surfaces.

You pass by the unobtrusive boundary sign that marks the start of the Glen Canyon National Recreation Area. Wyoming paintbrush (Castilleja linariaefolia) is the tall red plant. For the next four miles the wash meanders along. In the last two miles before the next side drainage, the passage constricts considerably.

A northern side canyon is quite choked with vegetation at its mouth, and remains like that for the first mile upstream. There are plenty of reasons for exploring this canyon. If you work your way upstream, you'll pass a pool at the base of the pouroff of the western arm. Just when the vegetation ceases, there's another pool that fills the space between the walls. This may require swimming. There's a short climb up the fluted shute and then the canyon floor opens into a sandy wash. A sandy overhang and a sudden dead-end complete the passage.

(An easier hike, which is also the route out to the Fence Canyon trailhead on the Egypt bench, is to climb up the west wall after you've thrashed through the first set of willows. The obvious break on the west side occurs just after the rockfall and you've waded knee deep across the backed-up water. Continue to climb as high as possible, so you can head two narrow steep side cracks.

Without straying too far from the rim, head north until you can look down the west arm. A short distance before it lips out, you can descend to the floor of the wash. Take a quick look at the lip of the pouroff and the pool below. It's an easier ascent up the other side of this side wash.

If you are hiking out to the trailhead, continue on the slickrock until you intersect the upper sandy part of this drainage. This wide, shallow wash occurs above the sudden dry waterfall. After heading west for a short distance, which is where you should intersect this wash, follow it when it turns north. When the ridges present a broken display to the northwest, contour around the eastern edge of those ridges. Then turn west until you hit the base of the Egypt escarpment and connect with the route up from Fence Canyon.)

Continuing down Twentyfive Mile Wash, one more mile brings you to the junction with Fox Canyon. Entering on the south side, this box canyon provides an exit route to the Early Weed Bench (Trail 25). This short side

Alcove, side canyon of Twentyfive Mile Wash

canyon is not named on the topographic map.

As the main canyon deepens, desert varnish adds additional color to the walls. The skyline is accentuated by sandstone domes. The walls are marked by horizontal cracks, where blocks have fallen away and arches are being formed. The streambed is eroding the softer Kayenta layer, leaving many good sandy benches for camping. Actually, there are benches at two levels, the one at stream level and an older mud bank twenty feet above you.

The next two southern sidepassages also box up. Another three miles of progressively deeper canyon brings you to the junction with the Escalante River.

TRAIL 24
FENCE CANYON

Difficulty: Strenuous
Length (one way):   3.5 miles
Time: 2 to 3 Hours
Maps: Moody Creek 15
Water: Fence Canyon

This is a short hike with outrageous views. The vista from the rim gives you a good idea of the difficulty of estimating distances and direction in this domed country. Since both arms of this canyon box out at their heads, a fence across the mouth makes this an excellent pasture. Luxurious growths along the flowing stream add to the array of colors found here. A three-day loop trip can be made by continuing down the Escalante River (Trail 21) and exiting along a northern arm of Twentyfive Mile Wash (Trail 23).

This trailhead is located at the end of the Egypt road, 9.1 miles east from the turnoff at the Hole-in-the-Rock road. The turnoff occurs 17.2 miles down the Hole-in-the-Rock road. There is a hiker register-box at the end of the road.

From the trailhead sign, pick up the trail switching down off the rim slightly to the north (left). When the trail reaches slickrock, steps have been chiseled into the rock. (This is also the stock route used by local ranchers.) After the first drop, the route seems to drop away into a series of pools. Contour south for about thirty yards on the somewhat more level sandstone until you see a narrow crack heading down. Follow the side of that crack down to the sandy wash. There may still be some chairns to guide you, but it's much better to take a route you feel safe and comfortable with.

Stay in this sandy wash until it starts to notch up and drop sharply. Then cross over, finding the most level route between the sandstone domes. The general direction of travel is in a northeasterly direction. Don't drift too far to the left. As you're walking over the sandy pockets, keep your bearings by staying in visual contact with the south arm of Fence Canyon on your right. There's a large alcove undercut on the south wall that is a distinctive landmark.

Continue east past the fence and down to the sandy bench that is the point above where the two arms come together. The north arm should be visible also. Angle right and down through the purple ledges. There are several paths that bring you down to the flowing water.

A well-worn path winds along the stream, sometimes climbing up a short hill to avoid a stream constriction. After nine crossings, the descent after the last little rise brings you to the junction with the north arm. This branch also has water flowing in it. Exploring upstream, stop after you've

Line camp, Fence Canyon

passed the first amphitheatre on the north wall. If you look high and to the left, a fair sized triangular arch should be visible just below the skyline. Passing several more alcoves on your trip upstream, the canyon comes to a beautiful, abrupt halt in another mile.

Continuing downstream past the union of the two branches, go through the gate blocking the path. When the path forks, the path climbing to the left leads to a cabin used by the cowboys and a view of the Escalante River. The right fork crosses the stream, goes through the fence against the south wall, and provides walking access to the river.

A challenging continuation is to follow the Escalante River down to the next western side canyon, walk up Twentyfive Mile Wash to its first northern tributary, and then negotiate the cross country route to the base of the escarpment of the Egypt bench. The route up to the trailhead is the same one you came down.

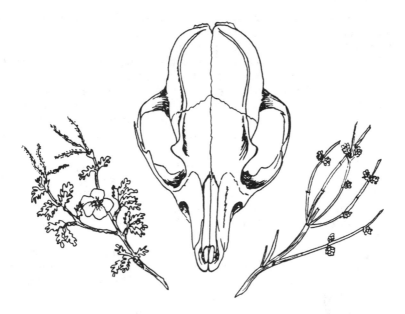

TRAIL 25
FOX CANYON

Difficulty: Strenuous
Length (one way): 2 miles
Time: 2 Hours
Maps: Moody Creek 15
Water: Bring your own

   This route down the edge of the Early Weed Bench brings you to the scenic lower portion of Twentyfive Mile Wash via a somewhat hazardous descent into Fox Canyon. This side canyon is worth total exploration. An exciting three to four day trip can be made by continuing down Twentyfive Mile Wash (Trail 23), along the Escalante River and up Scorpion Gulch with a five-mile cross country walk back to the car (Trail 26). An adequate map is essential for this hike.

   Fox Canyon is not marked on the topographic map. It is the first side canyon of Twentyfive Mile Wash inside the boundaries of Glen Canyon National Recreation Area. Proficiency in map reading and cross-country navigational skills are essential before attempting this hike. The next short side canyon east of Fox Canyon is a box canyon so care must be exercised to insure that you are traveling to the correct side drainage. Discuss this trip with the NPS rangers before attempting it.

The trailhead is reached by driving down the Hole-in-the-Rock road for 24.2 miles to the Early Weed Bench sign. Turn left and be ready for the sharp turn the road makes as it crosses the wash. Continue on for 5.3 miles. Be sure to watch the mileage in order to arrive at the correct place to leave your car. From the parking spot, a sandstone knoll is visible on the rim directly to the east. The road continues for another half-mile to a register box (Trail 26).

From the car hike due north and over the edge of the rim. Descend 60 feet to a ledge of sandstone that makes walking easier. Strike off in a northwesterly direction. The route descends the slickrock escarpment, dropping over 300 feet in three-quarters of a mile. Visible to the north are the steep walls of the lower portion of Fox Canyon where it joins Twenty-five Mile Wash.

As you look down toward Fox Canyon you will see a prominent butte with a brown top. The butte serves as a landmark to focus upon as you work your way across the rolling landscape. The vertical walls of the southeast arm of Fox Canyon are also visible.

Continue in a northwesterly direction to the head of the dry main arm of Fox Canyon. Follow the west rim of the canyon in a northeasterly direction. Don't stay too close to the rim because there is one little side branch which must be skirted. Continue along the edge of this little branch to where it drops abruptly into Fox Canyon. At this point it is necessary to cross the drainage.

Once you are on the east side of the drainage, there is a direct descent down the slickrock to a large, sandy bench. This is the tricky part of the route. Either a fifteen foot friction walk or a controlled slide gets you down to the sand. Locate the well-worn path that cuts back in a southerly (right) direction down to the floor of the canyon.

A couple of bends will bring you to the junction with Twentyfive Mile Wash. The first one lets you look up at the lip of the pouroff you recently crossed. Going up canyon, both the main arm and the southeast branch box up suddenly to end the exploration.

Sand dune entrance to Scorpion Gulch

TRAIL 26
SCORPION GULCH

Difficulty: Strenuous
Length (one way):   8 miles to Escalante River
Time: ½ Day
Maps: Moody Creek 15
Water: Bring your own and lower Scorpion Gulch

This exposed five-mile cross-country route should be tried only by the physically and mentally prepared.   The ability to negotiate a route across this uneven topography using the map and compass bearings is absolutely essential. Orienteering your way across open slickrock brings you to a sandslide that allows access to a very scenic side canyon of the Escalante River. Using this route as an exit, a loop trip can be made down Fox Canyon (Trail 25) and along the river (Trail 21).

The directions are the same as the previous hike except that you drive a half-mile farther to the end of the Early Weed Bench road. There is a trail register and plenty of room to park.

135

Arch on route to Scorpion Gulch

Scorpion Gulch

Before starting the hike, it is valuable to lay out the topographic map and acquaint yourself with the general features to the east. The first challenge is to circumvent the steeply eroded drainage patterns just below the rim. A short walk back up the road (north) provides access to the sandstone benches that border this broken area.

Head east, staying north of the promontory visible about two miles to the east. This is the first of several such landmarks that serve as orienteering guides. The route is a mixture of sandy areas interspersed with small sandstone knolls and ridges. Your route of travel should bring you just north of this outcrop. A small arch is visible near the top.

Cattails in Scorpion Gulch

After going around this feature, a sharp pointed butte becomes visible two and a half miles to the Southeast. It is the tallest feature on the horizon. This butte is identified on the topographic map as Coyote (VABM 5458) bench mark. To the east of this butte and on the other side of Scorpion Gulch, a flat-topped mesa stands out against the skyline. (Mesa is the Spanish word for table, and it accurately describes this geographical feature.)

Set a line of travel that will take you north of the butte and directly toward the mesa. The topography is quite broken near the base of the butte, so stay a half-mile to the north of this rock outcrop. Since it difficult to walk a straight line through this rolling country, it is necessary to frequently check and adjust your line of travel. An hour or two will bring you to the steep walled canyon of Scorpion Gulch.

Once you are at the floor, head downcanyon. In a mile you will come to a large sand dune straddling the canyon. Upon descending this sand dune, streamside vegetation begins to appear. Large overhangs have been eroded out of the walls in this portion of the Scorpion Gulch.

A half-mile farther water appears. Several large cottonwoods are growing in the bed where the water seeps out of the ground. Standing under those trees in the spring I was bombarded by the female catkins. Looking up I spotted the reason. Solitary vireos (Vireo solitarius plumbeus) were in the trees pecking at the seeds. The conspicuous white wing-bars and white eye-ring on this gray bird made identification easy.

It's a gentle walk along the stream until the northern side-branch joins. Another large overhang can be seen at the base of the Navajo layer. Now the Kayenta forms the base and sides of the stream. The resultant series of cascades and pools add to the colorful character of this canyon.

After the dry wash comes in on the right, the canyon heads northeast again. By this time the stream has cut through the softer Kayenta layer, and Wingate sandstone forms the walls of the canyon. There are two pools in succession where large rockfalls have made travel difficult. Both of these can be bypassed on the south side by picking your way through the fallen rocks.

Below the second pool, Scorpion Gulch has a verdure tone. Cattails and other riparian vegetation choke the banks. The rootstocks and young shoots of this plant were considered delicacies by Indians and the early settlers.

When you can see the free-standing pinnacles, you're at the river and the destination of the hike. There are several good campspots at the mouth, especially on the sandbar east of the stream.

TRAIL 27
DRY FORK
COYOTE

Difficulty: Strenuous
Length (one way):   6 miles
Time: 1 Day
Maps: Big Hollow Wash 7.5
Water: Bring your own

This day hike explores three narrow slots that drain the north side of Dry Fork Coyote Gulch. Peek-a-boo, Spooky, and Brimstone are challenging, claustraphobic, exciting, and fun. Caution must be exercised when the weather is warm because midget faded rattlesnakes (Crotalus viridis concolor) have been found in Spooky Gulch.

Follow the Hole-in-the-Rock road for 26.6 miles. The junction is not marked but there is another dirt road taking off directly opposite this one. Take the left hand turn and also both left forks you will come to later. This brings you to the turnaround in 1.7 miles.

From the turnaround where you park your car, walk north to the edge and start down. Almost immediately there are several little stairsteps in a natural crack that will get you below the ridge. Follow the wide sandy draw until it starts to drop sharply away. Work your way to the west side of the wash and drop down the sand dune until you're back in the wash. Stay in the wash until it intersects Dry Fork.

Exploring up canyon, it immediately slots up. Walking in the wash, the walls stay constricted for about a half-mile.

Down canyon, Peek-a-boo is the first defile coming from the north. You can climb up the short chimney right at the mouth if you have boots or shoes with good traction. The amount of water in the plunge pools will determine the extent of your further progress. After a couple more scooped out pockets, there's a double natural bridge. Further up the convoluted slot are two more small natural bridges. These carved out features give this slot its name.

When you hit the first wide sandy area, it's easier to go up and around on the right side. It's a serious squeeze for the next fifteen feet or so. Dropping back into Peek-a-boo it quickly becomes a senuous passage again. When the walls fade away, it becomes a very wide sandy wash.

I like the little climb at the mouth but you might want to do this passage from the top. Left of the mouth there is a sand dune that allows you to climb up so you walk the rim for a half-mile to the entrance at the upper sandy wash.

Narrows in Peekaboo Canyon

Natural bridge, Peekaboo Canyon

Spooky Gulch

Author in Spooky Gulch

Twisted Navajo sandstone, Dry Coyote Gulch

On down the main canyon, the next slot east is Spooky Gulch and it definitely lives up to its name. It likewise starts as a wide sandy wash about a mile up from its mouth. Cross-country travel similar to Peek-a-boo is required to get to that entrance. It is possible to go up this slot from the mouth but it requires a bit more scrambling.

Starting from the top, Spooky quickly walls up. There's a rock jam in the early portion, but a ladder has been left in place to aid in the six foot descent. You can crawl through the small natural bridge or go around it. From here down the passage progressively narrows. Most of time it is necessary to walk sideways with your daypack in your hand. The walls curve inward near the top, so only occasionally light shafts filter down.

From the head (top) of Spooky Gulch you can contour southeast for about three-quarters of a mile to a big sand dune that is the route down into Brimstone Gulch. The lower mile of Brimstone is a very wide open draw but it quickly narrows above the sandslide. It is very dark about a half-mile up the narrows and a cold-looking pool stopped me. The walls widened just enough that I couldn't bridge across it. Walking the western rim above Brimstone, it remains very narrow for at least a mile.

An easy return route is to walk up Dry Fork. There is a chockstone blocking the narrow stretch a half-mile up from the mouth of Brimstone Gulch. It can be climbed on either side. Or you can turn left before this narrow section and head up the pack trail shown on the map. It's an obvious route up the open arm. Once you're back on the rim it's a short cross-country walk to the car. (Instead of going up the open arm, you can swing off to the right and go over a low pass and back into Dry Fork and back up to the place you come in.)

There are more side slots to explore further down the Gulch. It is possible to go all the way down Dry Fork to its junction with Red Well, but it is a long walk.

TRAIL 28
RED WELL

Difficulty: Moderate
Length (one way):   6 miles
Time: 1 Day
Maps: Big Hollow Wash 7.5, King Mesa 7.5
Water: Coyote Gulch

Although not as popular as Hurricane Wash as a route to lower Coyote Gulch, this slightly longer hike (by .7 of a mile) is scenic and not as crowded. Wide benches are followed by a tight constriction. Several colorful side spurs add diversity. Campsites are numerous.

There is a BLM sign announcing the turn to the Red Well trailhead. This sign is 31.5 miles down the Hole-in-the-Rock road. Taking the left fork, a trail register appears in 1.5 miles.

The name Red Well came from an early sheepherder by the name of Ersell (Red) Shirts, who dug a well in the wash so that the sheep could have water. That actual location is south of this trailhead.

From the sign, pick up the path just to the north that immediately heads down to Big Hollow Wash. Coyote Gulch joins just to the right. At this point it is a dry, sandy wash.

A quick mile and a half walk and Dry Fork of Coyote Wash enters from the left. There may be some ground seepage but the water is not appetizing.

There are wide sandy benches above the stream with the sandstone walls off in the distance. The first side draw forces you down closer to the floor of the stream. A mile has passed by this point. Just before the next side spur drops in, the channel narrows and there is a huge log jam and a pile of tumbleweeds creating a barrier. Russian thistle is synonymous with images of the old west. This is the most common of the tumbleweeds. Introduced from Europe late in the nineteenth century, it has become a widespread nuisance. The stiff, prickly leaves and many branches makes it painful to walk through patches of the weed. Bypassing this obstacle on the north side, another set of narrows presents itself. It is easier to climb the southern bank to bypass this barrier.

The Park Service fence appears shortly after these challenges. The canyon starts to deepen and narrow and the colorful walls of Navajo sandstone are quite brown and tarnished.

The second fence is encountered after another mile of hiking. This fence is strategically located right after a short side slot and a bend in the stream.

After another half-mile, water enters from a northern side arm. There's a pseudo-entrance before a domed rock but the passage is just beyond. This

Sideblotched lizard

narrow side canyon is loaded with willow so it is a struggle heading up to explore. As you pass the dry waterfall on the right in about a half-mile, there are two large overhangs in the bends of the canyon. Another half-mile and the canyon boxes up.

Back down Coyote Gulch, small grooves of juniper dot the bends of the stream. After another two miles of easy walking, the canyon widens and a large stand of cottonwoods cover the bench. Directly ahead is a dry overhang that has several level campspots. Rain water poured over the northern edge one night we were there and it sounded as though it was roaring through our bedroom.

Another narrow side slot enters from the north. A quarter-mile stroll up this arm will bring you to a grooved pouroff. One spring the pools along this canyon were filled with strings of toad eggs.

There is a short narrow passage. The next side canyon coming in from the west is Hurricane Wash.

Waterfall, Coyote Gulch

Lobo Arch (Jacob Hamblin), Coyote Gulch

TRAIL 29
HURRICANE WASH

Difficulty: Moderately Strenuous
Length (one way):   13.2 miles to Escalante River
Time: 2 Days
Maps: Big Hollow Wash 7.5, King Mesa 7.5, The Rincon 15
Water: Hurricane Wash and seeps along Coyote Gulch

This is the easiest and shortest approach route to lower Coyote Gulch, the most popular hike in the area. A natural bridge, two arches, cascading waterfalls, deep overhangs, a sculptured streambed, and a rincon all add up to a very scenic canyon.

Use the Hole-in-the-Rock road log for the exact mileage. The signed trailhead appears shortly after a stock corral and cabin on the left side of the road.

There is a large parking area on the right side of the road. If you have a four-wheel drive you can go a quarter-mile down the wash and park by the trailhead. (The beginning of this road was washed out in 1984.) Hurricane Wash is open and sandy at this point.

145

It's a mile of walking before there is any indication of a canyon. The sand makes progress slow. Several small constrictions alternate with a wide wash. The wash remains dry for almost four miles. By now the walls have attained some height. Once water starts flowing from the spring, most people change to their tennis shoes.

A couple of sharp bends brings you to the National Park fence. There is a hiker's maze to pass through. This arrangement prevents cattle from passing by and solves the problem of gates being left open. Please use it. From here the springtime greenery accompanies you to the junction with Coyote Gulch.

There is water flowing in this drainage also. From here it is 7.9 miles to the Escalante River. There is a large sandy bench across the stream from the junction. This is the first of the many available campsites heading downstream.

After a couple of meanders, a small tributary comes in from the north (left). A short detour will add to your trip. When the alcove appears to the right, you can either continue at creek level or scramble up to the bench. Either route brings you to an amphitheater at the upper end, but the higher one gets you to the base of a dry waterfall.

As you continue down Coyote Gulch, water seeps start to appear along the walls near stream level. The bend before and the one by Lobo (Jacob Hamblin) Arch* are deeply overhung, with desert varnish streaks giving you an idea of the vertical relief. It's a fish eye view when you look up inside one of these bends. You can climb through the opening of this massive arch from either side.

Lobo Arch was named for a gray wolf which terrorized cattle in this area. He was the lone survivor of a pack killed in the House Rock Valley area of the Arizona strip in 1926. This wolf swam the Colorado River and migrated to the lower Escalante. Since this wolf had a curiosity about tin cans, a trap was set for him among a pile of cans. After dragging the trap for ten miles, Lobo was finally shot.

The first really usable water seeps appear on the fern-covered bank just past the arch. You stand in the creek and catch any of the several voluminous streams of water. A shallow overhang on the opposite bank makes a great place to camp.

One spring when we camped at this spot we were serenaded by the calls of the local toads. Because of the echoing affects of the canyon walls, the noise was overwhelming.

Spring colors continue along the stream. The tall red paintbrush (Castilleja chromosa) blend well with the exposed rusty colored Kayenta beds over which the stream passes. These scooped out pockets and narrow troughs first appear after four more bends.

---

*Following Edson B. Alvey's list of place names, this arch is called Lobo Arch. I agree with him by keeping the original names given by the settlers and early stockmen. Later name changes, even if they are placed on the topographic map, appear in parentheses.

146

Coyote Natural Bridge

The passageway constricts, then turns sharply through a narrow portal framed on the right by a rock pillar. The bend behind it is a rincon, a former meander of the stream.

One more bend brings you to Coyote Natural Bridge. The prevalence of coyotes in the whole region was the reason for the naming of the gulch and this natural bridge.

After you've gone another mile downstream, there appears to be a large domed rock blocking your path. There are two alternate routes available. If you look up to the cliff on the left, there appears to be an arch. This is actually just a dark hole.

Choice one goes up and over the saddle behind the rock dome. There is an excellent view of Jug Handle (Cliff) Arch from that saddle. Go left through the cottonwoods along the bank. There is a defined path up and to the right where the rock face is not smooth and sheer. After you start to descend on the other side of the ridge there are some grooves cut into the sandstone to indicate the way. The trail winds toward the waterfall and then switches back the other direction. It takes you back down to streamside.

The second choice is to stay along the water and follow it around the bend. At the far side of the domed rock, a rockfall has obstructed the channel. The first few blocks have to be bypassed. Then you cross to the right bank and locate the path that climbs up and around the worst part of the rockjam and the resultant waterfall. This trail stays high as it rounds the corner. There is another view of the arch. Directly below is a level, potential campsite. The trail slopes down and rejoins the stream.

Author's camp, Coyote Gulch

At the next bend is a water seep tucked against the south wall. This fern-covered seep will quickly fill your canteen. You can see that this water is running out at the contact point between the purplish Kayenta and the overlying Navajo sandstone.

Travel below this point becomes more challenging. You pass another rincon on the left. The first two waterfalls can be bypassed on the right side. After you pass the second one you have to step down the purple ledges to reach the stream again.

When the canyon turns east again just past the second waterfall, a thin waterfall comes off the north wall. A huge overhang that could sleep fifteen people greets you around the next bend.

You can carefully walk down the ledges at the edge of the next stairstep waterfall. The rate of descent appears quite steep through this half-mile because the Navajo cliffs have risen high above you. This section has a profusion of seeps on the north wall.

Having gone through the wiggles of the "W" (at least that is how it looks on the topographic map), the banks seem to disappear and the walls close in. Three rock cairns on the right side are set out perpendicular to the stream flow. These are indicators for the trail that climbs up the north wall and provides access to the Escalante River when the lake level is above 3700 feet. At this level it's impossible to continue down Coyote because the lake floods the mouth of this drainage. The cairned trail switches back and forth through the layered Kayenta beds and then levels out and heads east and around the neck of the promontory. To get a good view of Skyline (Stevens)

148

Arch, leave the trail and walk toward the edge of that point. The trail continues towards the north and then heads down the next little side draw to the river.

The other trail continues down Coyote Gulch. When you reach the area of the rock jam, leave the streambed on the right side and find the path that starts by a cottonwood tree and a big boulder. Juniper logs have been used to reinforce the trail and reduce eroison. The Crack-in-the-Wall trail continues straight up the hillside and goes between the rock domes visible to the south (Trail 30).

To continue down Coyote, go along the ledge by the rock cairn. There are some extra paths so stay on the lower one. This path traverses the sloping ledges. Cottonwood trunks have been placed against the wall to aid you in your ten-foot descent back to stream level. Another half-mile brings you to the mouth of Coyote Gulch.

Ladder, lower Coyote Gulch

TRAIL 30
FORTYMILE RIDGE

Difficulty: Strenuous
Length (one way):   2 miles
Time: 2 Hours
Maps: Sooner Bench 7.5, King Mesa 7.5, The Rincon 15
Water: Bring your own

This route provides access to the Escalante River or lower Coyote Wash. It is an exposed, cross-country walk and not recommended for summertime hiking. There are outstanding views of the Henry Mountains in the distance and domed buttes near the mouth of Coyote Gulch. The narrow Crack-in-the-Wall is an interesting route off the rim. This is a difficult route to locate. It is easier to find your way to a car left at the trailhead coming from Crack-in-the-Wall than to use this as an entrance route.

Follow the Hole-in-the-Rock road for 37.1 miles to a BLM sign which indicates the left hand turn on to the Fortymile Ridge road. Follow that road seven miles to the trailhead. The road is quite sandy, with deep sand the last two miles. You will pass two stock tanks on the left. Continue on to where the road bends sharply to the right. From here it is one half-mile further to a junction. Take the left fork, keeping up your speed through the deep sand, until you reach the trailhead. There is a register box at the trailhead.

From the trailhead, you can see the confluence of Coyote Gulch and the Escalante River. Take a compass bearing at this point so you can determine your line of travel. You want to end up slightly to the right of that junction. This landmark is not visible when you drop below the sandslide. Hike along the jeep trail down the ridge. Do not take the left fork, but continue on to the sandslide which will take you down to a gentler topography. There are no easily discernable landmarks on the horizon so a compass bearing is an eassential travel aid.

Another mile of slickrock walking in a northeasterly direction will bring you to the rim of the Escalante River. If you have drifted too far to the **south**, the steep walled canyon will be filled with the waters of Lake Powell. Although there is a cairn on the rim to indicate the location of Crack-in-the-Wall, the route is difficult to locate. The crack is very narrow and runs parallel to the canyon wall. It will be necessary to remove your pack and maneuver sideways to get through.

You will then find a huge sandhill below you. Follow the trail going down the sandhill heading north. Erosion is a serious problem so tread gently. This route brings you down to the saddle. Going north (or left) will bring you down to Lower Coyote Gulch. Good views of Skyline Arch

150

(Stevens) and the Wingate cliffs of lower Coyote Gulch are possible on the way down.

A right turn at this location will take you to the lower Escalante. However, you should stay on top of the Chinle ledges where you look down into the draw below. Where the ledges end, continue down into the drainage until the trail crosses over. Watch carefully for this crossing as you do not want to wander on down the draw where it dead ends at the cliffs above the river's edge. There are cairns to guide you through the broken pile of rocks out to the flat shelf of purple rock. Turn sharply south and follow the ledge past views of the two side drainages coming down on the opposite side of the river. Immediately after you pass the second one, the trail slopes down to the river level and you are at the end of this trail. If you wish to make a loop, you can travel upstream and turn up Coyote Gulch. This is dependent upon the lake level.

Author in Crack-in-the-Wall

151

Dance Hall Rock

TRAIL 31
DANCE HALL ROCK

Difficulty: Easy to strenuous
Length (one way):   1/16 of a mile
Time: ½ Hour to all day
Maps: Sooner Bench 7.5
Water: Bring your own

This historic outcropping of Entrada sandstone was used by the Hole-in-the-Rock expedition as a place to dance. The relatively smooth floor of the amphitheater made this a natural gathering spot. By climbing around the amphitheater, it is possible to explore the solution holes that have been weathered into the sandstone.

This historic site is also signed, 37.8 miles down the Hole-in-the-Rock road. The parking area is just off the road, with Dance Hall Rock visible directly ahead. It is an easy walk from the parking spot up to the open area of Dance Hall Rock.

The San Juan Mission camped for three weeks near Fortymile Spring just to the south. Serious road work was required to get from here to Hole-

152

in-the-Rock. As late arrivals joined the trek, the company spent some of their evenings dancing at this natural stage. There were three fiddlers plus other musicians, so they must have had a good time. With winter snow blocking the road back to Escalante, the decision was made to push on through the rugged country ahead.

There is plenty of open slickrock country to explore behind Dance Hall Rock. Careful friction walking up the sandstone slopes reveals an altered landscape. A variety of solution holes have been weathered into the sandstone. One of the deepest ones has enough soil in the bottom to contain a large cottonwood tree. Othes have filled in with sand and vegetation and look like miniature desert gardens.

Concretions

Grass, cottonwood, and slump block, Fortymile

TRAIL 32
FORTYMILE GULCH

Difficulty: Strenuous
Length (one way):   6 miles
Time: 1 Day
Maps: Sooner Bench 7.5, The Rincon 15
Water: Fortymile Creek

This highly scenic route gets more challenging as it progresses. The varied terrain and ever deepening walls make this a colorful hike. This hike contains a wonderful surprise. All of the side washes of this drainage presented steep barriers to the San Juan expedition as they built their wagon road toward the Colorado River.

There is no sign marking this trailhead so careful attention needs to be paid to the mileage log for the Hole-in-the-Rock road. Two miles past the sign to Fortymile spring the road dips into Carcass Wash. Since Fortymile is a box canyon, this route was chosen as an entrance. The name Carcass Wash was derived from cattle falling to their death when they tried to cross this narrow chasm.

The hike starts down the wash until you come to a gray pouroff. Stay on the bench on the south side for a quarter-mile. Carefully work you way down the sandy slope until you get to the floor of the wash. It is an easy stroll for the next mile to the junction with Fortymile Gulch.

The gulch is still wide at this point although the canyon walls in the distance are getting higher. After another mile of travel, the narrow slot of Sooner Wash comes in on the right. This is an exciting side defile to explore without a pack. Some chimneying techniques are necessary for climbing over the numerous large boulders that block this wash. (This route is not recommended as an alternate route back to the trailhead because of the scrambling involved in getting over these chockstones and some challenging climbing at the upper end.)

Further down Fortymile there are several deadend short draws that come in from the north side. Water appears right after you've passed the second side-draw. As you round the first bend after the water starts to flow, look for the portion of the cliff that has fallen away from the right wall. The route can either follow the stream or you can climb onto the large benches above the stream.

The stream angles to the north and it's time for another side excursion up the drainage heading due north. This easy walk has some finely-scooped-out water pockets where the erosional forces have been at work on an exposed sandstone slab. This side arm comes to an abrupt halt. The fluted pattern of this jump and the large sandy amphitheater that end this walk were inducements for exploring every side drainage I passed.

Author in water pockets, side canyon of Fortymile

Hidden waterfall, Fortymile

The twisting pattern and closed-in walls of Fortymile Gulch down stream from this side passage mark the boundary of Glen Canyon National Recreation area. The next bend brings the surprise. There's an easy route down the sand on the right.

Another two bends and it's time to start wading. The walls have seriously closed in at this point. A short passage where the water slides over bedrock is followed by a chockstone and deep wading. Stemming can get you through this first tight stricture but this technique is difficult with the weight of a pack. There are several of these spots where deep pools present an extra challenge. The canyon remains constricted and full of water until its junction with Willow Gulch, but there is one bend where a short climb up the south wall will bring you to a sunny, sandy respite.

Deadend side canyon, route to Broken Bow Arch

TRAIL 33
WILLOW GULCH

Difficulty: Moderate
Length (one way): 3 miles
Time: ½ Day
Maps: Sooner Bench 7.5, The Rincon 15
Water: Willow Gulch

This highly scenic short hike has a very impressive arch that protrudes majestically away from the canyon wall. The nature of the canyon changes quickly in its short course, with a luxurious growth of spring flowers along the lower walls. This hike can be combined with Willow Gulch (Trail 32) to make a challenging one or two-day loop trip.

A dirt road goes left diagonally from the Hole-in-the-Rock road in the flat area of Sooner Bench. The odometer reading should read 42.7 miles since leaving Highway 12. This side road deadends in 1.4 miles.

From the parking spot by the small water tank, you head down the sand dune slightly to the northeast. (Before starting down canyon, take a short walk up through the narrows. Just when it opens up, there is a hanging garden and cave on the north wall. Hanging gardens are a characteristic feature of the region, and are formed where there is water seepage along the horizontal bedding planes of the sandstone rocks. Such water-loving plants as maindenhair fern (Adiantum capillus-veneris), golden columbine (Aquilegia crysantha), and red monkey flowers (Mimulus cardinalis) usually can be found here.)

Going down canyon, there is another challenging set of narrows to negotiate. If you are claustrophobic, you may bypass these above on the south side.

The short side spur coming in from the south is recommended as a short side hike. Just past this junction, water starts seeping out of the ground. Another half-mile of walking brings you to the junction with Willow Gulch. This wash is walkable all the way back to the Hole-in-the-Rock road, but it loses character in a half-mile. That first half-mile is worth the exploration. There's a large alcove a quarter-mile up on the east side that is a perfect spot to sit and relax.

The flow of water increases with the addition of the spring just below the fork. The water cascades over the layered red rocks of the Kayenta Formation. There's one pool deep enough for a cooling dip.

The stream holds your attention until a massive arch looms up in front of you. In the class and style of Rainbow Natural Bridge, this large arm of sandstone projecting from the north wall is one of the scenic marvels of the lower Escalante Canyons. It was named Broken Bow Arch by local historian Edson B. Alvey because in 1930 he found an Indian bow underneath it. Photographers climb hills on either side of the canyon for a spectacular well-balanced photograph. Another treat awaits the spring hikers as they walk the undercut banks of the bend beneath the arch. White small-flowered columbine cover the seeps found there.

This gulch was named for the profusion of willows that grow along the banks. Here they add color and don't create a bushy jungle like those found along the main Escalante River.

Just before the union with Willow Creek, the canyon walls close in and it's time to wade. A chockstone causing a small dropoff is an easy climb. The water seasonally varies in depth from knee deep to over your head around the bend from this obstacle. The lake appears immediately below the junction of the two creeks.

Broken Bow Arch

160

TRAIL 34
FIFTYMILE CREEK

Difficulty: Moderately Easy
Length (one way):   4 miles
Time: ½ Day
Maps: Sooner Bench 7.5, The Rincon 15
Water: Lower Fiftymile Creek and Lake Powell

Although the lower portion of the canyon and Gregory Natural Bridge are under the waters of Lake Powell, the remaining canyon is a quiet retreat. A skyline arch, several overhangs, and a challenging walk to the waters of Lake Powell are highlighted features. Since the lower canyons are much less frequently visited, the wilderness nature of the canyons remain intact.

This is another hike that starts at a side fork instead of the head of the named canyon. The unsigned trailhead occurs 46.9 miles down the Hole-in-the-Rock road. Park by the geological bench mark (4237) on the left side as the road drops to cross another wash.

This unnamed drainage, opposite the projection of the Fiftymile Mountain known as Cave Point, is the start of the hike. The area around Cave Point is worth exploring. It is possible to walk down the whole length of Fiftymile Creek from where it crosses the road, but this route is shorter and more scenic.

This northern branch joins the other arm almost immediately. Reddish brown Carmel siltstones bound the wash. The first quarter-mile is a boulder hop. Just as the walls start to attain some height, there is an abrupt thirty-foot drop. There is an element of surprise in hiking a drainage for the first time that adds substantially to the excitement. Back up and climb up on the northern bench. Once on the benchland, go around the first rise on the right, cross the fence, and then skirt the second hill on either side. On the other side there is a friction walk down to the wash bottom. That takes care of the moderate part of the hike, it is an easy walk from here.

Once on the canyon floor, there is time to observe the patterns of desert varnish on the canyon walls. The bushes with the spiny holly leaves are Fremont barberry. The sudden loud whirl of a sage grouse (Centrocercus urophasianus) flying away is a heart stopper.

After two miles, the Fiftymile Creek drainage comes in from the right. At the junction, both arms have a similar appearance. The adventuresome can use this as a route back to the trailhead. (A mile up Fiftymile there is a side arm heading southwest. Take the right or north fork. This quickly becomes quite narrow with several chockstones to climb over. If you have a pack, a friend or a piece of rope will make it easier. Above the narrows, this becomes a sandy open wash. I climbed the ridge to the northwest and ended

161

Fiftymile Canyon

up where the two forks of the original draw come together just below the road.)

Continuing downstream after the Fiftymile junction, ground water and cottonwood trees appear. A mile below the junction, a prominent overhang is a beckoning campsite. (The sky was so dark and this shelter was so welcome that I didn't see the skyline arch until the following morning.) There are several more of these overhangs on the way down canyon.If shelter is not essential, there are plenty of campsites on the sandy benchland.

Just before reaching the lake, a short climb up the draw coming in from the north is rewarding. The sculpturing effects of water are a constant eye catcher. There was a Mexican freetailed bat (Tadarida brasiliensis) with a broken wing next to the stream. Bats unfortunately evoke images of vampires. I'm glad to see them darting around my campsite since each swoop means one less insect to torment me. Their specialized ability to navigate using echolocation makes it possible to hunt at night. The information received from their emitted supersonic sounds accurately allows them to capture small insects on the wing.

All along the canyon there is evidence of beaver, from the gnawed-through cottonwood trees to the marks of the branches being dragged along the sand. Beaver found in the Colorado River and its tributaries do not build domed stick homes or dams. They have adapted to the seasonal fluctuations of water by digging holes in the banks.

The final narrows before the lake are a challenge. The canyon narrows abruptly, turns sharply to the north, and a small boulder field has to be negotiated. The quicksand gets calf-deep through this section but the narrow channel draws you onward. Dead cottonwoods and a bathtub ring are reminders of a fluctuating lake level. It makes me wish I were older so that I could have seen the rest of these lower canyons before the lake covered them.

Nemo Arch

TRAIL 35
DAVIS GULCH

Difficulty: Strenuous
Length (one way): 5 miles
Time: 1 Day
Maps: Rincon 15
Water: Lower Davis Gulch

This canyon is the site of the mysterious disappearance of the young artist Everett Ruess. Davis Gulch has many attractions, among them a challenging overland approach, a steep stock trail as the entrance to the canyon floor, and a 100 foot arch. The remoteness of the country, a deep narrow gash in the earth, and lost Indian ruins and petroglyphs add to the romance of this canyon. Everett said in his last letter: "Often as I wander, there are dream-like tinges when life seem impossibly strange and unreal."

Fifty-two miles down the Hole-in-the-Rock road is the NPS sign for Davis Gulch. Park by the sign where the drainage crosses the road. Start hiking on the west side above the draw because it quickly slots up.

The route is a mixture of walking across slickrock domes and sandy

Author at entrance to Davis Canyon

pockets. Although the canyon can be used as a general guide, following the bends in the early part will make for unnecessary extra walking. There is also a narrow deep groove that comes in perpendicular to the main canyon in about a mile. You have to go around the head of this slot. If you like slots, take your pack off and head down this for a short distance. Confidence in your stemming technique is necessary since this tight corkscrew is difficult to walk in a normal manner.

The guide point to help you orient your way through this open slickrock is Fiftymile Point, a prominent projection off the Straight Cliffs behind you. Right after you've crossed this side crack, Davis Gulch heads in a northeasterly direction. The route from this point on is part of a stocktrail. Peeks into the narrow canyon are exhilerating. One view reveals a jump. (Footprints found below it indicate that there might be a way down, but it did not look exciting to me.)

If you've oriented correctly and are heading across the sandstone with an occasional visual contact of Davis Gulch, there is the space of three and a half miles of open cross-country walking. After wandering within the confines of canyon walls for years, there is a special feeling of freedom that comes from cross-country slickrock rambling.

At the first real break in the vertical walls, look east at the flat mesa top across the gulch and you will see a vertical cleft in the hillside. There are several rock cairns which warn you of the impending trail down. This is a stock trail used to bring cattle into the canyon. Follow along the side of the shallow depression until you're on the slickrock again. Locate the next rock cairn slightly to the right. If you lose the zig-zag route and go too far northeast, you can look down to where logs are piled close to the base of the cliff. That is the end of the stock trail. There are steps cut in the rock just before the bottom.

Once you are on the canyon floor there is a well-worn path leading downstream. Campspots abound. Depending on the water level, the lake should not be more than three bends down canyon. A lot of history is buried under the waters of Lake Powell.

Everett Ruess' thoughts help generate a sense of balance. Just a couple of short quotes from that other wanderer — "the wild silences have enfolded me, unresisting" — "I, too am singing in my heart, and I sing the song of the wilderness."

Heading up canyon, Nemo (Bement) Arch leaps out at you. Climb up the rubble and from inside, it will appear even more massive. If you continue upstream, the water stops flowing and Davis Gulch becomes a sandy wash. The mouth of the slot that was skirted on the rim is visible on the west wall, but there does not appear to be a way to climb into it. Several more bends and the canyon constricts tightly into a scramble route. Then a short walk brings you to the pouroff.

Davis Gulch was the last known campsite of the young artist Everett Ruess. His burros were found but his body and outfit were never recovered. This occured in the fall of 1934, when Everett was just 21 years old. Everett had been exploring the southwest for several years, sketching, making blockprints and writing poetry. His disappearance remains a mystery.

TRAIL 36
CLEAR CREEK

Difficulty: Moderate
Length (one way): 2 miles
Time: ½ Day
Maps: Rincon 15
Water: Bring your own

This cross-country route leads to views into Clear Creek, a box canyon. Although Cathedral in the Desert is under the waters of Lake Powell, the views from the rim of the canyon are impressive. The dramatic and sudden drop of this side canyon, hidden from view until you're right up on it, is typical of this broken country. An ability to read the lay of the land and a topographic map is essential before you wander off on this hike. There is no trail of any type and the walking is across open, sandy country.

This trailhead is not signed. When you have gone 55.3 miles on the Hole-in-the-Rock road, pull over to the side and park. From the side of the road, head north toward the center of the Henry Mountains visible on the skyline. The route is bounded by the hill immediately to the west and the green-lined mesa to the northeast.

Cross-country trekking allows you to set a gentle pace, picking a way that is defined by the rolling nature of the land. In this loose sand, contouring around dunes is usually easier than struggling over the top. There is plenty of time to get acquainted with the widely spaced plants of the Northern Desert Shrub Association. The finely haired, narrowleaf yucca (Yucca angustissima) needs to be approached with caution. The tips of the leaves are very sharp. The fruits of this plant were eaten raw, roasted, or dried for winter.

Stay on the slickrock to the south when there is the first indication of a drainage. A transverse side slot coming in from the northwest is a key landmark. The wash quickly drops away over a dry waterfall. Staying high on the slickrock you can look over the rim of the next pouroff. Following the bend of this already deep, narrow canyon, you come to the edge of a shallow alcove cut into the southern wall. A couple of bends of the convoluted course are visible to the northeast.

Keeping those same landmark hills as your guideposts, retrace your steps to the vehicle. The map has incorrectly marked Cathedral in the Desert. A cavernous cul-de-sac, the Cathedral in the Desert was so named because the streaks that strained the walls of this overhung grotto gave the appearance of being draped with long slender pennons (narrow flags born on lances).

Hole-in-the-Rock

TRAIL 37
HOLE-IN-THE-ROCK

Difficulty: Moderate
Length (one way): ¼ mile
Time: ½ Hour
Maps: The Rincon 15
Water: Bring your own

Although the bottom two-thirds of the original route has been flooded by Lake Powell, the upper third remains. This was the most challenging section, with remnants of the construction still visible. This site recognizes the important role pioneer determination played in early Mormon colonization. There is an excellent view of Cottonwood Canyon across the lake.

Drive fifty-seven and a half miles to the end of the Hole-in-the-Rock road. Use the Hole-in-the-Rock road log to identify features along the way.

From the parking area at the end of the road, go east to find the commemorative plaque bolted into the sandstone. The route down starts in the notch immediately to the south. Rockfalls have made the passage more interesting, but they do not create any real barriers. A short way down, steps have been cut into the sandstone. This is known as Uncle Ben's Dugway. Besides cutting steps and creating a shelf, holes were drilled lower down and parallel to the shelf. Stakes were driven into these holes; logs and brush were piled up to provide a track for the outside wheels. The wagons were then safely taken down this improvised road.

From the bottom of the dugway, it is a gradual descent to the lake. When you get to the water's edge, look back up at the route taken in 1880 by 250 people and 80 wagons. The amazing thing is this portion of the trek was considerably easier than some of the obstacles encountered on the east side of the river.

Andrew P. Schow and Reuben Collet had explored the country southeast of Escalante and took "an improvised two-wheeled cart" down the Hole-in-the-Rock. These early Escalante settlers played an important role in determining the route taken by the San Juan Mission.

The primary reason for the San Juan Mission was to establish better relations with the Indians. Converts from the Southern states were also looking for a place to live that had a warmer winter climate than their settlement in Colorado. The Mormon Church also wanted settlers to inhabit the border land as a buffer against encroachment by stockmen from Colorado.

The whole expedition was on the move for six months. It took a month and a half to enlarge the original Hole-in-the-Rock and construct a road three-quarters of a mile down to the Colorado River. When they finally reached the San Juan River, just east of Cottonwood Wash, they were just eighteen miles from their intended destination at Montezuma. They were too exhausted to continue. The site they settled is now known as Bluff. This incredible journey remains a milestone in the annals of western settlement.

This route was used for another year as the main road between the two settlements. Charles Hall operated the ferry at the Hole-in-the-Rock crossing for the rest of 1880, when the lack of traffic caused him to move to a more favorable site at the mouth of Hall's Creek.

Steps in Hole-in-the-Rock

TRAIL 38
BARKER RESERVOIR

Difficulty: Easy
Length (one way):   3.5 miles
Time: ½ Day
Maps: Barker Reservoir 7.5
Water: Bring your own

This short loop trip brings you in contact with six lakes and is also recommended for children. These lakes are stocked with trout, so the trip can be a fishing excursion. A side trip will take you through The Gap and on top of the Escalante Mountains.

Use the road log at the start of this section. Go west of Escalante to the Main Canyon junction. The North Canyon road branches off to the right almost immediately. Seventeen miles up this road brings you to Barker Reservoir.

Barker Reservoir has a primitive Forest Service campground that serves as an excellent base camp. This area has road closures to reduce erosion. Vehicles are only allowed on the road to Barker and Lower Barker Reservoirs. Since all the lakes are within two miles, this poses no hardship and allows for a leisurely stroll. This hike just taps the surface of what is available in this area. Other hikes can be planned with the help of the display map.

The trail takes off at the north end of the campground on the east side of the reservoir. There is a trail register in .4 of a mile. To do the loop hike, take the left fork to Flat Lake. The blazed trail stays in the woods and suddenly there is Flat Lake, tucked against the edge of Escalante Mountain. This ten-acre, shallow, grassy lake is stocked with brook trout.

At the next trail junction, a short side trip will take you to Blue Lake, a misnomer if I ever heard one. A buck mule deer (Odocoileus hemionus) was having a drink when I arrived. This half-acre lake also is stocked with brook trout. The main trail skirts the southern edge of Yellow Lake, six acres in size.

The next trail junction has a sign that says Clayton GS. 3. A left here will take you on a moderate trail up through The Gap. A mile hike up this trail will bring you along the edge of North Creek and into wide expansive meadows. The trail joins the road, then forks left for a half-mile to the guard station. Clayton spring receives critical acclaim for some of the best tasting water around. As the trail runs along North Creek, there is a fence and gate. It is as easy to climb over the boulder next to the gate as it is to go through the gate. Just as the trail emerges into the meadow, the wet, west arm provides most of the water. The meadows are lined with spruce trees, the state tree of Colorado. The bark is grey, and the cones are longer than the similar Engelmann spruce (Picea engelmannii). The color of the foliage is dark green, with only the edge of the new growth exhibiting the blue color. Yellow-bellied marmots (Marmota flaviventris) are found among the boulders in the meadows.

If you decide not to take the above jaunt, continue straight to the gate. The trail that continues east from here is called the high line trail and goes to Hog Ranch Spring where it connects with the John Allen Bottom Trail. Go right on this side of the gate and follow the faint trail along the fence. Very shortly it will angle to the southwest. Blaze marks on the trees will bring you to Joe Lay Reservoir. This shallow four-acre lake also has brook trout but weeds make fishing difficult. The route had been dotted with mushrooms. These add color but only the experts should pick them.

Stay on the east side of the reservoir until it joins a jeep road. Follow this road until it hits a "T." The route becomes a trail again heading southwest through the trees. The main trail skirts Lower Barker Reservoir on the north and closes the loop at the trail register. Follow the trail along Barker Reservoir back to the campground.

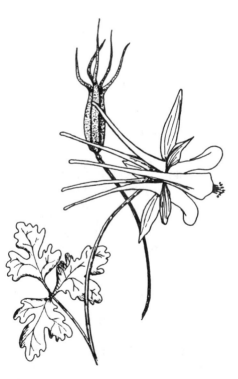

TRAIL 39
POSY LAKE
LOOKOUT

Difficulty: Moderately Easy, recommended for children
Length (one way):   ½ mile
Time: ¾ Hour
Maps: Posy Lake 7.5
Water: Available at the campground

This short 400-foot uphill walk takes you to a viewpoint that offers a wide vista. The profusion of wildflowers along the way turns this into a nature walk.

Head up the Hell's Backbone road for 13.9 miles to the Posy Lake junction. Two miles on this road takes you to the campground. The signed trail starts next to campsite number 10.

A short steep climb takes you around the hill and up to a small roofed platform. To the east, the sandstone cliffs of Pine Creek stand out in bold relief against the spruce and pine forest. Further east, the Henry Mountains captivate the skyline. (These laccolithic mountains were first described by Grove Karl Gilbert of the then newly formed U.S. Geological Survey. Laccoliths are dome-shaped intrusive structures. In a modern re-examination of the Henrys, Charles Hunt concluded that the laccoliths were fed by a central stock that intruded up through the overlaying sedimentary rocks. This configuration of a central stock and spready laccolithic branches resemble cacti with arms. These isolated mountains, named the Dirty Devil Mountains by A.H. Thompson, were discovered in 1872 by members of the second Powell expedition when they traveled overland to retrieve a boat left at the mouth of the Dirty Devil River.)

On a clear day, the Abajo or Blue Mountains can be seen further east. Navajo Mountain, also a laccolith, stands along to the south. This peak is sacred to the Navajo Indians.

Wandbloom penstemon (Penstemon virgatus) is a pale violet flower found along the trail. This flower is unique in that the tongue-like stamen is not hairy like in the rest of the penstemons. The low shrub Gamble oak is also much in evidence. (William Gamble was a young ornithologist who came out west with Thomas Nuttal in 1844. He discovered about 100 new species but the rigors of frontier life did not agree with him. Contracting typhoid in a winter crossing of the Nevada desert and the Sierra Nevada Mountains, he was buried at Rose's Bar, California. Not even his bones found any rest because they were sluiced down the hillside when the forty-niners discovered hydraulic mining. The acorns of the oak named after him are avidly eaten by wild turkeys and squirrels while mule deer browse the green foliage.)

Returning from the lookout, a short side trip down the west slope of the hill brings you to a shallow green lake. Continue along the open area to the south and the first of the Tule Lakes comes into view. These shallow ponds are duck havens. Return by the same route to the trail.

The chattering noise coming from the trees belongs to the spruce squirrel (Tamiasciurus hudsonicus fremonti). You are made well aware of the fact that you have entered this small animal's territory. The short tail and black stripe at its side are distinctive. These energetic workers help perpetuate the forests by storing pine cones in the soil.

TRAIL 40
JACOB'S RESERVOIR

Difficulty: Moderate
Length (one way): 5.4 miles
Time: 1 Day
Maps: Big Lake 7.5, Jacobs Reservoir 7.5
Water: Pine Creek, Barney Lake, Jacob's Reservoir

This trail is an excellent combination of hiking through the woods and high alpine meadows. A variety of wildlife can be spotted on this hike. This long drainage goes through quite a transformation before it joins the Escalante River. The Thompson party went up this stream to circumvent the canyons of the Escalante.

Take the Hell's Backbone road north to the Blue Spruce campground turnoff. Go past the campground for another 1.3 miles. Pull off next to the big boulder on the left. There is a new Forest Service sign on the tree marked Auger Hole Lake — 2 miles.

The trail follows the old road and immediately crosses Pine Creek. At the end of the first open meadow you come to an old wooden tent structure. Now the trail climbs up the hill. The junction of the Auger Hole Lake trail is signed and continues left up the hill. The trail going right is signed Jubilee G.S. #107 and also heads uphill but does not climb so quickly. This is the way to Jacob's Reservoir. The trail contours around the hill, crossing two small streams. The second of these is Pine Creek.

After continuing around the hill the trail seems to run out. There are lots of downed trees in the way. This is the edge of a timber sale. A skid road is evident. Going slow through these obstructions, the next blaze mark is uphill, to the left, and back the way you came. In other words, the trail jogs and then climbs steeply along the side of the hill. There are openings between the trees and the surrounding hills are visible. The trail finally levels off.

When the trail and Pine Creek join together again, the stream is bounded by rock out-croppings. This constriction is utilized by the cattlemen to divide grazing areas. Be sure to close the gate after passing through. The trail runs briefly alongside the water and then crosses it. Climbing again, the trail has been rerouted several times to avoid erosional damage. The general direction is clear. Skirting a large meadow on the right side, there is an old sign on a tree that says Shurtz Ranch. That is about all that remains of this early ranching operation. The trail stays on the right side of the meadow and climbs up to a saddle. Here you are greeted by two large built-up rock pillars, the one on the left has a telephone pole held in place by the rocks. This line ran from the Jubilee Guard Station, which is a rustic cabin just to the left of the trail. A new shingled roof offsets the darker cabin walls.

The trail climbs sharply until it opens up into a boulder strewn meadow, crossing through an old log fence. In late summer there is a good chance of seeing mule deer grazing among the cows. The cairned way leads you into the meadow and then turns abruptly southeast until you can see Pine Creek. It is not necessary to follow the cairns exactly as long as you angle into the meadow to the right. The route turns to the northeast and runs along the creek until you can see Barney Lake against the talus slope. The trail continues along the west bank of Pine Creek until there is a small rise. The cairns take you over the rise and away from the creek. Wandering through the next stretch of meadow, the creek is still visible to the east.

The next rise is the dam of Jacob's Reservoir, where a yellow-bellied marmot has made a home among the boulders of the dam. (The name marmota comes from the Dutch name of the European species of woodchuck. This ground dwelling mammal is the largest rodent native to the Southwest. This animal occupies a tremendous altitudinal range and is found from the ponderosa pine community to above timberline. Its loud warning whistle is a familiar sound in these high meadows. It hibernates through the long winter months.)

The trail crosses the dam and winds around the east arm of the reservoir until it joins Forest Road 107.

TRAIL 41
EAST BOULDER
CREEK

Difficulty: Moderately Easy
Length (one way): 7.1 mile loop
Time: 1 Day
Maps: Grover 15
Water: Various unnamed lakes, E. Boulder Creek

This pleasant loop trip has plenty of wildflowers. The view of the Boulder Mountain escarpment at the halfway point is striking. The walk is through a mixture of meadows and wooded areas, with plenty of accessible water. Beaver dams are a highlight. A side trip to Trail Point provides superlative views and is well worth the steep climb.

Continue north on Highway 12 past the Anasazi State Park for 5.2 miles. Turn left at the Garkane Power Plant sign. When the road forks, go right up the King's Pasture Road for 6.7 miles.

Although you can drive right to the trailhead sign, there are several good places to camp where the road branches and heads east. The sign to Trail Point and rock cairn just past the junction on the west side of the road is the exit point. Since the recommended hike is a loop, parking here will put you back at your car at the end of the day. Walk east up the road, passing the sign to Deer Creek Lake.

The low plant with the fernlike leaves and a small cluster of white flowers is western yarrow (Achillea lanulosa). Very similar to the imported eastern species (Achillea millefolium), the western species is native. It is named after Achillis, who reportedly discovered the healing properties of this member of the sunflower family. The Zuni applied the leaves to the skin to produce a cooling sensation.

Stay on the main road heading north rather than the faint tracks turning uphill to the left. The road climbs gradually and is bounded on the left by an old log fence. To the right is a Forest Service sign indicating the start of the trail. Although it is numbered 115 on the F.S. map, no numbers are visible on the sign. The blazed trail winds through the aspens as it climbs up the hill.

When the trail forks, follow the blazed route left and through the fence. The other trail continues to Grass Lake and dead ends. The trail drops down to East Boulder Creek and stays on the east side of the stream. It crosses several small secondary rivelets and then climbs steeply. A profusion of wildflowers grow along these brooks; especially striking is the tall dark-blue columbia monkshood (Aconitum colubianum). This flower is

177

Beaver dam, Boulder Creek

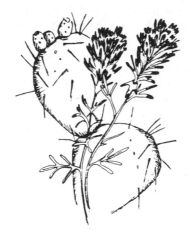

similar to larkspur, but can be differentiated by the helmet shape of the upper sepal. All species of monkshood contain poisonous substances.

The trail wanders through the aspens and spruce trees, opening suddenly to a small lake contained by a beaver dam. I saw several families of anglers trying their luck at this pond. The trail is dotted by red Indian paintbrush. (They do look like someone dipped them in a paint bucket.) That red display consists of bracts, the flowers are white and inconspicuous.

After winding along the ridge for a short distance, the trail abruptly switches back and down the hill. This grassy lake is part of the headwaters of Boulder Creek in the summer when no more water is draining off the Aquarius Plateau. This unnamed lake is ringed on the north and west by straight volcanic cliffs and talus slopes. This escarpment is part of Boulder Mountain, the eastern end of the Aquarius Plateau. The trail crosses the beaver dam at the southern end of the lake and then heads southwest through stands of aspen and small meadows. Ducks can be heard in the rushes, but they are well hidden. Golden columbine and harebells (Campanula rotundifolia) line the lake's edge. You can retrace your steps at this point but the loop trail connects you with a challenging side trail and some different scenery.

When the trail breaks through the trees and the stream reappears to the east, follow the blazes along the western edge of the meadow. The trail turns to the west at the edge of a section of private property when the house becomes visible in the distance. Within a half-mile you come to the northeast corner of Divide Lake, marked by a Forest Service sign. Here a strenuous 1.7 mile side trip will take you to the top of the plateau and some striking vistas. The path going to Trail Point heads around the north side of the lake and turns abruptly to the right in about 150 feet. There is a "T" and an arrow pointing to the right, blazed into an aspen on the left side of what appears to be an old road. There is a log placed across the track marks. Look for the blazes and a fairly well-worn path.

The trail goes over a short rise and then skirts a very shallow pond. There are two large volcanic rock cairns to help get you through this meadow, since the cattle paths can make the way confusing. Head north past the point of the escarpment. The trail turns west and a long, steady, steep climb will bring you to the top of the ridge.

Walk out on the boulders to the edge of the outcropping for an expansive viewpoint. West Boulder Creek is below you to the west. If your eyes follow it upstream, they will see a beautiful two-tiered waterfall where the creek cuts through the edge of the plateau. Contrasting sandstone buttes and the green area of Salt Gulch lie to the south. The East Boulder Creek drainage that you just left is directly to the east. The trail continues along the top of the plateau to Spectacle Lake, which can also be reached by Forest Service Road 162.

To complete the Boulder Creek loop, stay along the edge of Divide Lake and then head southeast down the drainage. The trail skirts the south side of the fence and is marked by a huge cairn before it crosses the road. The trail stays along the fence, then heads north and crosses Boulder Creek. On the other side it climbs the hill. Carefully cross the water pipeline that supplies the Garkane Electrical Plant. Old blaze marks on the aspen lead you east up the hill and back to the road.

Beaver Lodge

TRAIL 42a DEER CREEK LAKE

Difficulty: Easy
Length (one way): 3.7 miles
Time: 1 Day round trip
Maps: Grover 15
Water: Gresham Spring, Deer Creek Lake, Green Lake

This trail winds through a series of aspen groves and meadows to a 22 acre lake. A beaver dam located in the unnamed lake to the west of Deer Creek Lake is an added attraction. With very little elevation change this hike is an easy stroll through the woods.

Follow the directions to the road junction at the end of the King's Pasture road from the last hike. Just before the road deadends at the forked gate, go up the road that forks right for .2 of a mile. The trail is signed. Follow the blazes down and to the right instead of the old road that goes due east. The small shrubby plant with yellow flowers and five leaves is a bush cinquefoil (Potentilla fruticosa). This member of the rose family is heavily browsed by deer.

The well-worn trail winds through standing aspen groves and, with an occasional opening to an area of blowdowns, southern vistas. Some of the aspen are quite large, and the scars on the trunk create a visual contrast to the smooth white bark. Aspen are trees that can quickly occupy an open area created by some disturbance in the forest. Many of the sprouts can originate from a single root system creating a uniform appearance. The name quaking aspen comes from the fluttering sound generated by the stems of the leaves. The brilliant colors generated by these trees are the epitome of a western fall.

After about an hour, the trail skirts the northern edge of a meadow. Chris Lake is visible about a half-mile to the south. Boulder hop across the creek. Ignore the jeep road and continue to the right as the trail crosses the second stream.

Now the view opens up to the north as the spruce trees abut the volcanic escarpment of Boulder Mountain. The trail stays at the edge of the meadow and then skirts the southern end of an unnamed pond. Look for the beaver home in the middle of the pond. At the first cairn, stay along the shoreline and don't take the track that lies just to the south. After two more cairns, the trail takes off straight through the woods. Look for the blaze on the tree and don't take the path that curves northeast. The path passes right by Gresham spring, a verdant spot. When the trail leads into a big open

Aspen on Deer Creek Lake trail

meadow, the route is marked by a pole and a cairn to the east-northeast. Following these guides across the meadow you will intersect an old jeep road and F.S. sign. Follow the road .2 of a mile north to Deer Creek lake.

Go around the west end of the lake and scramble over the boulders up to Green Lake. This narrow and deep lake is surrounded by boulders and a talus slope on the northwest side. This is a great swimming hole late in the summer if you want to really cool off. This is the only lake I explored that resembled the cirque lakes found in the Rocky Mountains.

Green Lake

TRAIL 42b
DEER CREEK LAKE

Difficulty: Moderately Easy
Length (one way): 2.7 miles
Time: ½ Day
Maps: Grover 15
Water: Deer Creek Lake

This hiking trail to Deer Creek Lake is a mile shorter than trail 42a. The dirt approach road is also shorter and less bumpy. The trail follows an old jeep road that climbs steeply through meadows and trees. A panoramic view is available if you turn around a short distance up the trail. Deer Creek Lake is a good spot for bird watching.

Continue north on the newly paved road from Boulder. There is a Forest Service sign on the left hand side of the road indicating the turn to Deer Creek Lake. The sign is 11.1 miles north of the Anasazi State Park in Boulder. The signed road from the highway is bumpy in spots but brings you to the trailhead in a half-mile. Take the right fork to the sign.

The trail follows an old jeep road which immediately starts up the hill. The trailhead sign is surrounded by wild rose bushes. Following the jeep road, the ground cover is quite open and by turning around you have an expansive vista to the south. Immediately below you the green fields around Boulder are contained by white slickrock meses. Navajo Mountain is the dominant dome far to the south.

Ground cover consists of dandelions and snakeweed (Gutierrezia sarothrae). This light-green member of the sunflower family has a woody base. Clusters of small golden yellow flowers cover the entire plant. If this plant is abundant it is considered an indicator of overgrazed land, especially by sheep. The name "snakeweed" is derived from the fact that when a sheep is bitten, a poultice is made of the ground and boiled leaves of the plant. This is reported to reduce the swelling and save the sheep.

In a mile there is a hiker's registration box. The trail has climbed the whole time up to this point. It's always fun to read the comments people have written.

Directly ahead are two shallow depressions that are natural water holes for the cattle grazing in the distance. Passing these boulder-strewn depressions, the trail climbs sharply into the trees. Now you are back in that familiar pattern of spruce and aspen commonly found at this elevation. The first time the trees thin out there is another set of small shallow ponds on either side of the trail.

A golden-mantled ground squirrel (Spermopholus lateralis) scurried away at my approach. It is larger than the chipmunks, without the facial stripes. Instead, the entire head is a coppery color. Their behavior is not as frantic as chipmunks, preferring more open country for foraging. Hibernating in the winter, the summer is spent storing food, breeding, rearing the young, and laying on fat for the next cold stretch.

Climbing over one more short rise, the path leads into a very large meadow. The pole off to the west is the trail marker of the Deer Creek Lake trail coming from E. Boulder Creek (Trail 42a). The two trails come together at the Forest Service sign. From here, another two-tenths of a mile takes you to the west end of Deer Creek Lake. The aspen at the edge of the meadow were alive with common flickers. This redwinged bird has an easily distinguishable flight pattern of alternating wing beats and gliding.

Detour off the jeep road to the east along the faint path that leads to the south shore. The better part of a day can be spent observing the ducks swimming and feeding among the reeds. There is a path of sorts along the shore. When you see the beaver house, there is a campsite to the south that is used by fishermen. It has a built-up fire ring and a primitive but usable toilet facility. Part of the primitive definition comes from the fact that the door is missing. It was later found as part of the superstructure of a raft.

Negotiating the path along the shoreline requires stepping over the fallen trees. Chipmunks and junko create a flurry of activity to mark your progress. Continuing east along the shore, you run into a patch of wild raspberries (Rubus idaeus). I stopped eating long enough to enjoy the dramatic volcanic escarpment that lines this placid lake.

REFERENCES

NATURAL HISTORY

1. Arnberger, Leslie P., Flowers of the Southwest Mountains, Southwest Parks and Monuments Association, Globe, AZ, 1974.
2. Brown, Vinson, Charles Yokum, and Aldene Starbuck, Wildlife of the Intermountain West, Naturegraph Company, San Martin, CA, 1958.
3. Burt, William H., and Richard P. Grossenheifer, A Field Guide to the Mammals, Houghton Mifflin Company, Boston, 1976.
4. Crittenden, Mabel, and Dorothy Tefler, Wildflowers of the West, Celestial Arts, Millbrae, CA, 1975.
5. Elmore, Francis H., Shrubs and Trees of the Southwest Uplands, Southwest Parks and Monuments Association, Globe, AZ, 1976.
6. Hayward, C. Lynn, D. Elden Beck, and Wilmer W. Tanner, Zoology of the Upper Colorado River Basin: I. The Biotic Communities, Brigham Young University Science Bulletin, Biological Series, Vol. 1, No. 3, Brigham Young University, Provo, UT, 1958.
7. Murie, Olaus J., A Field Guide to Animal Tracks, Houghton Mifflin Company, Boston, 1974.
8. Nelson, Ruth, Plants of Zion National Park, Zion Natural History Association, Springdale, UT, 1976.
9. Olin, George, Mammals of the Southwest Mountains and Mesas, Southwest Parks and Monuments Association, Globe, AZ, 1961.
10. Patraw, Pauline M., Flowers of the Southwest Mesas, Southwest Parks and Monuments Association, Globe, AZ, 1977.
11. Peattie, Donald C., A Natural History of Western Trees, Bonanza Books, New York, 1953.
12. Peterson, Roger Tory, A Field Guide to Western Birds, Houghton Mifflin Company, Boston, 1961.
13. Rabkin, Richard and Jacob, Nature in the West, Holt, Rinehart and Winston, New York, 1981.
14. Stebbins, Robert C., A Field Guide to Western Reptiles and Amphibians, Houghton Mifflin Company, Boston, 1966.
15. Welsh, Stanley L., Flowers of the Canyon Country, Brigham Young University Press, Provo, UT, 1971.
16. Woodbury, Angus M., Ecological Studies of Flora and Fauna in Glen Canyon, University of Utah Anthropological Papers No. 40, Glen Canyon Series No. 7, University of Utah Press, Salt Lake City, 1959.

GEOLOGY

1. Baars, Donald L., Red Rock Country, Doubleday, Garden City, NY, 1972.

2. Barnes, F.A., Canyon Country Geology for the Layman and Rockhound, Wasatch Publishers, Salt Lake City, UT, 1978.
3. Hintze, Lehi F., Geological History of Utah, Brigham Young University Press, Provo, UT, 1973.
4. Rahm, David A., Reading the Rocks, Sierra Club, San Francisco, CA, 1974.

ARCHEOLOGY

1. Ambler, J. Richard, The Anasazi, Museum of Northern Arizona, Flagstaff, AZ, 1971.
2. Barnes, F.A., and Michaelene Pendleton, Canyon Country Prehistoric Indians, Wasatch Publishers, Salt Lake City, UT, 1979.
3. Wormington, H. M., Prehistoric Indians of the Southwest, Denver Museum of Natural History, Denver, CO, 1947.

GENERAL HISTORY

1. Abbey, Edward, and Philip Hyde, Slickrock: The Canyon Country of Southeast Utah, Sierra Club, San Francisco, CA, 1971.
2. Breed, Jack, First Motor Sortie into Escalante Land, National Geographic, Vol. 96, pp. 369-404, 1949.
3. Chidester, Ida, and E. Bruhn, A History of Garfield County, Garfield County News, Panguitch, UT, 1949.
4. Crampton, C. Gregory, Standing Up Country, Alfred A. Knopf, New York, NY, 1964.
5. Crampton, C. Gregory, Military Reconnaissance in Southern Utah, 1866, Utah Historical Quarterly, Vol. 32, No. 2, pp. 145-161, 1964.
6. Gregory, Herbert E., Scientific Explorations in Southern Utah, American Journal of Science, Vol. 243, pp. 529-549, 1945.
7. Henderson, Randall, When the Boats Wouldn't Float – We Pulled 'em, Desert Magazine, September, pp. 5-13, 1950.
8. Le Fevre, Lenora, Boulder Country and Its People, Art City Publishers, Springville, UT, 1973.
9. Miller, David E., Hole-in-the-Rock, University of Utah Press, Salt Lake City, UT, 1966.
10. Moore, Robert, W., Escalante: Utah's River of Arches, National Geographic, Vol. 108, pp. 399-418, 1955.
11. Porter, Elliot, The Place No One Knew: Glen Canyon on the Colorado, Sierra Club, San Francisco, UT, 1963.
12. Rusho, W. L., Everett Ruess: A Vagabond for Beauty, Peregrine Smith Books, Salt Lake City, UT, 1983.
13. Woolsey, Nethella G., The Escalante Story (1875-1964), Art City Publishers, Springville, UT, 1964.

Rudi Lambrechtse

BIOGRAPHICAL SKETCH

Born in Holland, I immigrated to this country with my parents in the 1950s. Family summer vacations brought an early appreciation for the tremendous variety this country had to offer. This wonderlust remains as a central aspect of my character.

Western exploration continued after completion of a B.S. degree, until all fifty states, Canada and Central America had been visited. Caught up by the space and wide diversity of the intermountain west, the last ten years have been focused here. Backpacking, riverrunning, crosscountry skiing, and photography have all deepened my understanding of the land.

A break was taken to complete a Master's Degree in Biology at Northern Arizona University in 1982. The last two summers have been spent as a trail guide in Grand Canyon National Park. I plan to continue a career in ecological awareness.

I started hiking in the Escalante Canyons in 1972. Breaking my foot on my first hike did not deter me, it's remained a regularly visited area. A total of 750 miles were hiked for this book.

I've been an avid outdoor photographer for twelve years. Trying to get past just recording an area, my interest is focused on form and texture photos. I've had several shows in Flagstaff of my work.

Notes: